What I Wish I'd Known in High School
The Second Semester

I love the youth of the Church. I have said again and again that I think we have never had a better generation than this. How grateful I am for your integrity, for your ambition to train your minds and your hands to do good work, for your love for the word of the Lord, and for your desire to walk in paths of virtue and truth and goodness.
—President Gordon B. Hinckley

What I Wish I'd Known in High School
The Second Semester

by John Bytheway

Deseret Book Company
Salt Lake City, Utah

Library of Congress Cataloging-in-Publication Data
  Bytheway, John, 1962–
    What I wish I'd known in high school : the second semester / John Bytheway.
      p.   cm.
    Includes bibliographical references.
    ISBN 1-57345-095-2 (pbk.)
    1. High school students—United States—Religious life.
  2. Teenagers—United States—Religious life. 3. Christian life—
  Church of Jesus Christ of Latter-day Saints—Juvenile literature.
  4. High school students—Conduct of life. 5. Teenagers—Conduct of
  life. I. Title.
  BX8643.Y6B99   1995
  248.8'3—dc20   95-36686
                                                                     CIP
                                                                     AC

Printed in the United States of America

10 9   8   7   6   5   4   3   2

To John Peay, my priests quorum advisor and friend, who magnified his calling and helped many of us in the Parley's Second Ward survive our teenage years.

Acknowledgments

Thanks to my family, my absolute favorite people in the world. Thanks also to Russ and Colleen Peterson and family for letting me wear out their fax machine, and to Milt and Helen Sharp for their friendship and encouragement. My gratitude to the wonderful staff at Deseret Book—Sheri Dew, Emily Watts, Shauna Gibby, Kent Ware, and Tonya Facemyer. And a special thanks to Elder M. Russell Ballard, who told us to get back to work.

Class Schedule

Orientation

Welcome Back!

Hey, everybody! How have you been? It's good to see you! I mean—uh—it's good to *write* to you! Wow, here we are again; can you believe it? Another book called *What I Wish I'd Known in High School,* but this time it's (drum roll, please) *THE SECOND SEMESTER!* (Cymbal crash.) Yes, friends, it's back-to-school time. It's time to take another exciting excursion on the Starship o' Knowledge, to learn new things, to think new thoughts, to boldly go where few teenagers have gone before. (I tried to arrange for an F-16 flyover at this point; let's see, how would that sound? Ffffffffff—no, that's tearing up a piece of paper; let's see, F-16s. . . . How about Rrrrroooor—no, that sounds like my stomach before lunch; SSSSSSHHHHHHH—no, that's a librarian. Okay, forget that part. Just imagine four F-16s flying overhead and being very loud and exciting, and imagine the pilots screaming, "Yeeeeeeeehaw!" as they pass by.)

Anyway, I'm glad you're back. It will be fun to talk with you again. There is so much to learn and explore and discover, and you, my fellow explorer, can do it all because you can read! Books are like mini-time machines that can take you wherever you want to go. I love the power of books. (You know, new books *smell* good, too. Go ahead, stick your nose in here and take a whiff. Isn't that nice?) So I guess we ought to make the same deal we did last time, okay? Read this instead of watching TV, and I'll do my best to make it more interesting, more exciting, and more testimony building than prime-time ever was. Is that a deal? Deal.

As you may know, last year Deseret Book and I produced

a book called *What I Wish I'd Known in High School: A Crash Course in Teenage Survival*. It was a really fun experience, but something was missing. By the time I finished writing, I realized I had left so many things out—good things, important things! So this time, I've written about all *those* things and called it *The Second Semester.* And it's going to be fun. But it's also going to be a little more personal.

Let me explain. No, there is too much. Let me sum up. Once I attended a fireside. A wonderful talk was given, and there was a peaceful, thoughtful spirit in the chapel. Everyone in attendance was "turned inward": people were sitting quietly, thinking about personal, spiritual things. You know the feeling—I know this has happened to you. It was very interesting because the closing hymn was over, the closing prayer was said, but no one left. The dance was starting in the other room, but no one wanted to leave the chapel! The overwhelming feeling shared by everyone in the room seemed to be, "I want to soak this feeling in for a few minutes." It was written on every face. People whispered to one another. No one told them to whisper; they just did. Why do you suppose that was? The music began to play in the gym, but no one seemed to care. Some even got a pained look on their faces when they heard the music start, kind of a "well, back to the real world" look. *I love it when that happens!* I love it when the youth notice the difference between the feeling of the Spirit and the feeling of the "Top Forty." (I get that same "back to the real world" feeling every time I leave the temple and go back to my car.)

Now, here's the problem. A few youth still had unanswered questions. Important questions. I know they did, because it was written all over their faces. A few of us stayed in the chapel and talked. We had a wonderful discussion while the majority of the group jumped around in the gym.

There are some questions that people ask only when they are on that deep-down level. That's where those young people were. They wanted to know about heaven, about Heavenly Father, about Jesus. Some of them weren't sure what they wanted, except that they wanted more—more of that sweet feeling that seemed to stay in the room. They had a wonderful case of "celestial homesickness." Some of those great teens had questions that they didn't want to ask in front of the others. (I wonder how many questions about important things don't get asked because people are too afraid.) Would you like to know some of their questions? How about this one: "How do I repent?" Wow. Is that an important question, or what? A little more important than which fork to use on a date, isn't it? How about this one: "How do I know if I've felt the Spirit?" and, "How can I feel it more often?" I can't tell you how thrilled I was, having lived a few more years but remembering my teenage years like they were yesterday, to sit with those five or six young people and talk about the weightier things of the gospel for the next two and a half hours. I think I would rather do that than attend any youth conference dance, or any amusement park, or any movie, anytime.

Well, my friends, I've tried my hardest to find answers to the deep-down questions and put them in this little book. I'm giving you fair warning, because there may be times when you look up from the pages and say, "Wow. This is serious stuff!" And it is. I don't know much myself, so I've looked for answers in the scriptures and from the words of the prophets. If I missed any of *your* deep-down questions, those are the best places for you to look too.

Anyway, your mom will be so pleased that you're reading something beyond the scholarly *TV Guide*. You'll learn some doctrine, but we'll have some fun, too. Yes indeed, we'll take a lunch break and have some laughs. I promise.

Let's get to work! Put this book down, go get a high-lighter, your scriptures, and a favorite beverage, and let's read. You might even want to take the phone off the hook.

(Right, like you or anyone you know would really take the phone off the hook.) Anyway, turn off the TV and read, and I'll try to make it as interesting as I can.

Well, that's it for Orientation. *It's back-to-school time!* First period is about to start—I'll see you in class!

Motivation 101
The Three Attitudes

And they were all young men, and they were exceedingly valiant for courage, and also for strength and activity; but behold, this was not all—they were men who were true at all times in whatsoever thing they were entrusted.

—Alma 53:20

You know the story. You may have even lived the story. Big family leaves on big trip and leaves something big behind. It's happened to your family, it's happened to my family, and it happened to Lehi and Sariah and their family. "Oh, great. We traveled two hundred miles, but we have to go back and get the plates. You know, the brass ones. Boys, would you please go back and get the plates?"

What's the difference between Nephi and Laman and Lemuel? Notice the different responses to exactly the same request. The "attitude brothers," Laman and Lemuel, say it's too hard: "It is a hard thing [you] have required" (1 Nephi 3:5). (Our generation would probably ask, "Is this gonna be fun?") Nephi, however, says, "I will go and do" (1 Nephi 3:7). Same request, opposite attitudes.

In fact, as you go through the Book of Mormon, you'll find that Laman and Lemuel usually ended up doing the same things Nephi did—they just had a bad attitude about it. That "little" difference, that difference in attitude, seemed to be passed down through many generations who felt they were "wronged in the wilderness," and it ended up affecting the destiny of both the Nephite and Lamanite civilizations.

No one wants to be labeled by others. But whether we like it or not, we label *ourselves* by our attitudes and actions. Laman and Lemuel labeled themselves, Nephi labeled himself, and every day we label ourselves by the things we say and do.

But, hey, let's be fair. I mean, hello, walking—no, not driving, *walking* two hundred miles to go and get something (from someone who doesn't want to give it to you), and then walking another two hundred miles to bring it back is a pretty huge request! We might even call it, uh, inconvenient. Yes, four hundred miles round-trip is a long way, which makes Nephi's "I will go and do" response even more impressive. But it's not just the big things that show what's inside of us. We also tell on ourselves by the little things we do. President David O. McKay shared this interesting little poem in general conference back in 1969:

> *You tell on yourself by the friends you seek,*
> *By the very manner in which you speak,*
> *By the way you employ your leisure time,*
> *By the use you make of dollar and dime;*
> *You tell what you are by the things you wear,*
> *And even by the way you wear your hair,*
> *By the kind of things at which you laugh,*
> *By the records you play on your phonograph.*
> *You tell what you are by the way you walk,*
> *By the things of which you delight to talk,*
> *By the manner in which you bury deceit,*
> *By so simple a thing as how you eat.*
> *By the books you choose from the well-filled shelf;*
> *In these ways and more you tell on yourself.*[1]

As you know, earth life is full of rules, requirements, commandments, dress codes, honor codes, Morse codes, and so on. When someone starts explaining the rules, an amazing thing happens. Watch how people respond! People begin to "tell on themselves" by their reactions. You'll see obedient, "I-will-go-and-do" types; whining, "It-is-a-hard-thing" types; and everything in between. For now, we're going to narrow the field down to three different groups or attitudes. Yeah, that's it, we'll call them the "three attitudes." (You've heard of the *beatitudes?* Well, these are the *three-attitudes.*)

HOW BAD CAN I BE?

I once attended a morality lesson during which anonymous questions were gathered in a shoebox and submitted to a panel of leaders. One of the questions, to our surprise, was, "How far can you go before you have to see the bishop?" Whoa. Nice attitude. Stated another way, the question was, "How bad can I be?" I guess this person wanted to know exactly where "bad" began so he or she wouldn't miss out on anything. A youth asking "How far can I go before it's bad?" is like a skydiver asking how close he can get to the ground before he has to open his parachute. The person who asked that question didn't realize that where "bad" *really* begins is in the heart, with a bad attitude, which reveals itself through bad behavior.

One way people show their membership in the "How-bad-can-I-be" group is by their strong reactions to things like dress standards, which are simply an attempt to draw the line on what is acceptable. They want to know exactly where that line is. For instance, they want to know exactly where the knee begins, or where "long hair" begins, so that they can get as close to being in violation of the code as possible and still be admitted to the dance. They may be secretly excited when they can "get away with" something, because that's the attitude: "What can I get away with?"

They tell on themselves another way by choosing music and entertainment that are right on the line as well. They say, "It wasn't that bad," or "I've seen other movies with a better rating that were worse." Once again, they live right next to the danger zone, not realizing that the most dangerous thing is the attitude itself.

They may say things like, "Hey, nobody's perfect"—which is true, but they're not trying to be perfect. They're not even trying to be good! They want to know how bad they can be. Elder Richard J. Clarke commented:

> Those who excuse transgressions by saying, "Well, I'm not perfect" may be reminded that conscious sin is a long way from perfection. We would do best to consider this counsel of President Brigham Young.

"Be . . . as perfect as [you] can, for that is all you can
do. . . . The sin . . . is [not doing] as well as [you
know] how" (JD 2:129–30).[2]

If you were to ask someone with this attitude why they
attend church or seminary, they might respond, "'Cause I
have to do this, I *have* to do that. They see life
as a big set of unfair rules, and obedience is an inconve-
nience and an irritation. Very un-Nephi.

HOW GOOD ARE WE SUPPOSED TO BE?

The next group wants to know, "How good are we supposed to be?" At first, that attitude might sound okay. But it
isn't! Stay with me, and I'll tell you why. Members of this
group want to do what they're supposed to do. In fact, if
you asked them, "Why do you go to seminary?" they would
say, "'Cause I'm *post* to." (Some people pronounce the word
"supposed" as "post.") These are good people, honorable
people. They do what they're "post" to, go to church and
attend meetings. They're willing to be good. Good for them.

And, hey, being good is good! But that's all it is—good.
It's not great, it's not valiant, it's just, you know, good. Sister
Ardeth Kapp said:

> It has been my observation, and it is my confession
> as a former participant, that many people drift along
> with the crowd in the Church. Many *good* people
> drift to sacrament meeting and Sunday School, even
> family home evening, and they drift through a casual
> study of the scriptures. . . . [They] step into the main-
> stream, getting deeply involved with Church activity
> and floating with the current, comfortable with a
> sense of false security that they are in the right place.[3]

"See, here I am, bein' good, doin' what I'm post to. Call
me the post-man, 'cause I do what I'm post to." Yup. It's
good to be good, but it's better to be *better* than good.

Now, here's the problem. Sometimes, for this group, being good has its limits. They wouldn't want to go too far. I once challenged a group of teens to give up a certain prime-time soap opera. We discussed the thirteenth Article of Faith, "If there is anything virtuous, lovely, or of good report or praiseworthy, we seek after these things." After realizing that many television programs failed to fit in those categories, most of the youth present willingly accepted my challenge. Others sat quietly, telling on themselves by the attitude written all over their faces. The message coming through loud and clear by their expression was, "I want to be good, but I don't want to be *that* good." Ouch! Did you catch how dangerous that is? Yes indeed. Heaven forbid we become *too* good—we might get too many blessings. Elder Carlos E. Asay told the young men in the priesthood session of general conference:

> There is a lie—a vicious lie—circulating among the Latter-day Saints and taking its toll among the young. And it is that a "balanced man" is one who deliberately guards against becoming too righteous.[4]

That's a lie I've heard myself, many times. It's not only false, it's very dangerous. When we want to be good but not *too* good, we may think we can choose which rules to obey and which not to obey. I'm not sure why, but every time I read the following quote to an audience, they laugh. I guess Elder Joseph B. Wirthlin shows us how silly "selective obedience" really is. Either that, or the laughter is the nervous giggles of the guilty.

> They claim to be obedient to God's commandments but do not feel at all uncomfortable about purchasing food at the store on Sunday and then asking the Lord to bless it. Some say they would give their lives for the Lord, yet they refuse to serve in the nursery.

The Savior spoke very explicitly about people who "draw near to me with their mouth, and with their lips do honour me, but have removed their heart far from me."[5]

After the last part of the quote, no one is laughing. Now, don't misunderstand, being good isn't bad, being good is good! But President Ezra Taft Benson said we need to be more than just good:

We have too many potential spiritual giants who should be more vigorously lifting their homes, the kingdom, and the country. We have many who feel they are *good* men, but they need to be good for something—stronger patriarchs, courageous missionaries, valiant genealogists and temple workers, dedicated patriots, devoted quorum members. [Okay, here's my favorite part:] In short, we must be shakened and awakened from a spiritual snooze.[6]

When was the last time you used the word *snooze?* Right! You were describing to someone how hard it was to get up one morning, and you explained how you kept hitting the snooze button! President Benson uses a powerful metaphor: spiritual giants in a spiritual snooze. Too many people continually hit the snooze button on the clock radio of their personal spirituality. "I'll be better someday, but for now, I don't wanna be too good, I'll just snooze. Someday I'll start a scripture study program, someday I'll say my daily prayers, someday I'll do what I'm post to, but not now. I'll just snooze for a while."

Aaagh! When are we going to WAKE UP? Sorry, I got carried away for a minute there. Anyway, back to the point. If we don't want to be in the "How-bad-can-I-be" group, or the "How-good-am-I-post-to-be" group, then where should we be? It's time to talk about the third attitude, and you, my friend, know all about this group. It's the group where you can find fine teenagers like you.

I WANT TO BE VALIANT!

I love this group, and I'll bet you're in it! This group doesn't ask, "How bad can I be?" They have absolutely no interest in what is bad. And *good* isn't enough for them, either. They want something better than simply good. Their question is on a higher plane: "Is it *valiant?* I want to be valiant. Is it better than average? Is it high quality? Is it extra-milc? Is it high class? That's where I want to bc. That's where I *belong.* I want to be valiant." No one has to remind these young people about rules. No one has to tell these young men they need a necktie at the sacrament table, or these young women exactly where their knee is. They carry their desire to please God everywhere they go. It is constantly burning inside. Like the others, they tell on themselves. The quality of their spirits shines brightly through their attitude.

Valiant people have no problem with dress codes. They usually agree with them. And even if they don't agree, they follow them anyway. That's the way valiant people are. They're more interested in being obedient than in knowing all the reasons for the rules. Oooh, that sounded good, can I say that again? *They're more interested in being obedient than in knowing all the reasons for the rules.* They get up on Sunday morning and think to themselves, "What should I wear today? Let's see, I go to church to worship the Lord. What does the Lord deserve? He deserves the best. Yeah, that's it. Sunday best." Valiant young women dress carefully because they realize they can attract young men in one of two ways: to themselves, or to their bodies; to who they are inside, or to how they look on the outside. They also realize that inner beauty is more, yes, more powerful in the eternal scheme of things than external beauty will ever be.

If you were to ask an "Is-it-valiant" person, "Why do you go to seminary?" they would give you that "what-a-strange-question" look and answer, "Because *I want to.* I want to learn, I want to understand, I want my testimony to grow." And when they get to seminary, they stay awake, and they stay focused. They don't expect to be entertained. They expect to learn! And they don't just listen to their instructor, they *help* their instructor by being actively involved in the class. They are always a part of the solution, and never a part of the problem.

"Is-it-valiant" teenagers are missionaries from the moment they get up in the morning. They preach a sermon in everything they do, and their attitude radiates to everyone else. You can feel it when you're around them. Just being in their company makes you want to be better. President David O. McKay said:

> Every man and every person who lives in this world wields an influence, whether for good or for evil. It is not what he says alone; it is not alone what he does. It is what he is. Every man, every person radiates what he or she really is. . . . It is what we are and what we *radiate* that affects the people around us.[7]

You just can't hide it when you're valiant! It radiates! "Is-it-valiant" teenagers become excellent full-time missionaries, too. Mission presidents love them! Their desire to do right comes from inside. These elders and sisters work hard and obey mission rules, not because they have to, or because someone's watching, or because they're post to, but because they *want* to. There's no casual study of the scriptures for them. They *hunger* and *thirst* after righteousness and after knowledge (see Matthew 7:7). They can't get enough!

If you were to ask an "Is-it-valiant" person, "Why do you go to church?" they'd answer, "Because *I want to.* I want to be clean. I want to be valiant. I love Jesus. He is so wonderful. His life was so amazing. I want to think like him, and act like him, and be like him."

If you want to be valiant, and you need a model to follow, think about Jesus. Jesus was a teen at one time. We have hardly any information about his teenage years. All we really have is summed up in one scripture: "And Jesus increased in wisdom and stature, and in favour with God and man" (Luke 2:52). But imagine you were able to go back in time, and you traveled back to Nazareth. Who's the first person you would look for? Let's say you were walking along a dirt road, and you met a young man. He was, say, sixteen or seventeen years old. He had dark eyes and auburn hair, and he was wearing typical clothes from that time. You stopped him to get directions and asked, "May I know your name?" He looked at you and answered, "My name is Jesus."

Think how this particular teen would have "radiated." Wow. If you ever wonder how to live your life, think about being the kind of young person Jesus must have been. He would have been valiant—obedient to his parents, a good worker, and kind and respectful to everyone. Valiant people focus on the Savior and try to live the words of a favorite Primary song, "So, little children, let's you and I try to be like him, try, try, try."[8]

Did Jesus ever ask, "How bad can I be?" or "How good am I supposed to be?" Did he do things because he had to, or because he was supposed to? Let's ask President Howard W. Hunter: "He was perfect and sinless, not because he had to be, but rather because he clearly and determinedly wanted to be."[9]

Why is it so important to be valiant? Do you really want to know? Our answer is in the scriptures. Explaining who will inhabit the terrestrial kingdom, the Doctrine and Covenants states: "These are they who are *not valiant* in the testimony of Jesus; wherefore, they obtain not the crown over the kingdom of our God" (D&C 76:79; emphasis added).

Wow. I guess being valiant is pretty important. Like Nephi, Laman, and Lemuel, you will find that much of your life and your eternal destiny will be determined by your attitude. We'll talk more as this book continues about being valiant, about having our hearts changed so that we sincerely *want* to be valiant, all the time. And now that you've been introduced to the three attitudes, tuck them away in your mind because we'll be referring to them again.

We'll close with an appeal from President Howard W. Hunter:

> We must know Christ better than we know him; we must remember him more often than we remember him; we must serve him more *valiantly* than we serve him. . . .What manner of men and women ought we to be? Even as he is.[10]

Well, you've told on yourself again, because you just finished First Period. You must be reading this book because you *want* to. You must be one of those valiant ones, because you want to learn! So, my fellow Nephi, let's go on to Second Period—not because we have to, or because we're post to, but because we want to.

FIRST PERIOD ENDNOTES

1. David O. McKay, Conference Report, October 1969, p. 87.
2. Richard J. Clarke, *Ensign,* May 1991, p. 42.
3. *Woman to Woman: Selected Talks from the BYU Women's Conferences* (Salt Lake City: Deseret Book, 1986), p. 53; emphasis added.
4. Carlos E. Asay, *Ensign,* May 1992, p. 41.
5. Joseph B. Wirthlin, *Ensign,* November 1992, p. 35.
6. *Teachings of Ezra Taft Benson* (Salt Lake City: Bookcraft, 1988), pp. 403–4; emphasis added.

7. David O. McKay, *Man May Know For Himself,* Clare Middlemiss, comp. (Salt Lake City: Deseret Book, 1967), p. 108.

8. *Children's Songbook* (Salt Lake City: The Church of Jesus Christ of Latter-day Saints, 1989), p. 55.

9. Howard W. Hunter, *Ensign,* November 1976, p. 19.

10. Howard W. Hunter, *Ensign,* May 1994, p. 64; emphasis added.

Spiritual Health 101

Hand Soap and Heart Transplants

I say unto you, can ye look up to God at that day with a pure heart and clean hands? I say unto you, can you look up, having the image of God engraven upon your countenances?

—Alma 5:19

If you were to look up the term *Service Project* in the dictionary of Latter-day Saint jargon, it might look something like this:

Service Project—*Sur'* • *vis Proj'* • *ekt* (Mormon): 1. An event usually advertised as "something really fun, but we're not going to tell you what it is." Followed by, "Wear grubbies and show up at the church. P.S. Bring a shovel." The *Service Project* is usually followed by a beverage and/or pastry (see *Refreshments*). 2. A few members may moan when hearing *Service Project*, but they always end up enjoying the experience.

One summer, I found myself involved in one of those service projects in San Antonio, Texas. About a hundred of us were busy painting a widow's home. We were having a good time. It's amazing how quickly you can get a major job done when there are a hundred people doing it. The "Is-it-valiant" group were working their hearts out, the "How-good-are-we-post-to-be" group were doing what they were post to, and the "How-bad-can-I-be" group were telling on themselves by playing around with the water hose. I was three or four rungs up a ladder painting one side of the house. (People driving by thought, "Hey, it must be the ladder-days." Ha, ha.)

Anyway, I was painting near the rain gutter, which I accidentally bumped kinda hard with my hand. Apparently the rain gutters hadn't been cleaned in a while, and bumping them showered my face with dirt and dust. I closed my eyes just in time, but the dirt went everywhere else, and I looked like I had been bobbing for potting soil. With the sleeves of my T-shirt I wiped the lovely combination of dirt and perspiration from my face. Yuck. By the way, did I mention how incredibly hot and humid it was that day? I didn't? Well, it was incredibly hot and humid that day. But I kept painting, because I knew there was a high-pressure shower and a big bar of deodorant soap in my future.

Things got worse before they got better. I continued to paint, finding in my path what looked like a vacant wasps' nest. It wasn't vacant. After my paintbrush sideswiped the nest, everything went into slow motion. "Willie the Wasp" did not appreciate having his mud porch freshly painted, so he flew out and landed on my hand. I remember thinking, "Oh, lookie there. There's a wasp on my hand." Then he stuck his little behind *in*, not on, the back of my hand. I thought to myself, "He's gonna sting me." (Aren't I quick?) He did. And it hurt. In a reflex action, I let go of the brush, which, on its way to the ground, hit a member of the teachers quorum squarely on the back. I felt awful. I stepped off the ladder, face filthy, hand throbbing, and apologized up and down to the young man whose shirt I had just ruined.

But we weren't done yet. Now we had to paint the metal bars around all the windows with a coat of black enamel. That was fine, except that I have a problem: whenever I'm working with a liquid, I always seem to get it on my hands. I remember when I was a kindergartner, whenever my family had pancakes for breakfast, the syrup would somehow magically creep up my fork and knife and get on my fingers. One morning at school someone asked, "Did you have pancakes for breakfast?" (I guess they could smell the syrup.) "No," I responded, "that's my new cologne, 'Evening of Maple.'" (Just kidding.) I learned while I was still young to wash my hands often so that I wouldn't carry the aroma of my most recent meal everywhere I went.

So now we're painting with black paint, and you can guess what happened. Yes, it crept up the brush and got all over my hands. Black paint. On my hands. Gross. When we arrived, the house was a mess and we were clean. Now we were a mess and the house was clean. All we did that afternoon was transfer messes! And I for one was anxious to transfer my mess again to a paint-thinner rag and a hot shower. Try to imagine it. It's hot. It's humid. Drops of perspiration and muck drip freely off my face, my T-shirt is soaked and filthy, and my hands are sticky with half-dried black paint. I was looking forward to a shower like it was the celestial kingdom.

What if the youth conference chairperson had stood up at that point and announced, "Brothers and sisters, we don't have time for you to take a shower before the fireside. Your clean clothes have been taken to the changing rooms at the church, and we'd like you to go straight there and put on your clean white shirts and your fresh clean dresses. Wear them over your filth and sweat, and go directly to the chapel for the fireside."

How would that make you feel—sitting there with clean, fresh clothes but feeling gross and sweaty and dirty underneath? Remember that feeling for a second, okay?

One time, when I was in college, I had to give a priesthood blessing at about 5:30 in the morning. A sister in my ward was really sick. We got dressed quickly and ran over to her apartment. My roommate did the anointing, and then it was my turn. I remember placing my hands on her head and then pausing. For whatever reason, I remembered the lyrics of a song my dad used to play on Sunday mornings. I remembered especially the chorus: "He that hath clean hands, and a pure heart." I looked it up later. The chorus is the answer to a question:

> Who shall ascend into the hill of the Lord? or who shall stand in his holy place?

He that hath clean hands, and a pure heart. (Psalm 24:3–4)

As I stood over this young woman with my hands on her head, I wondered, Are my hands clean? Is my spirit filthy and gross in any way? *Do I really have the priesthood today?*

That [the rights of the priesthood] may be con-ferred upon us, it is true; but when we undertake to cover our sins, or to gratify our pride, . . . the heav-ens withdraw themselves; the Spirit of the Lord is grieved; and when it is withdrawn, Amen [or, "that's the end"] to the priesthood or the authority of that man. (D&C 121:37)

I reviewed my life for a moment. I thought about my sins, about my attempts to repent and change, about the purity of my heart and motives, and about my prayers the night before. *Have I looked at a magazine that has stained my hands? Have I pushed a video into the machine that has soiled my spiritual fingers?* You young men will do this every time you're asked to give a blessing. Every time.

It is a wonderful feeling to go through this thought process, look at your hands, and think, "I'm okay. I can do this." It's a wonderful feeling when you're asked to break the bread at the sacrament table to know that your hands are clean. It is wonderful to kneel before the ward and hear the words "O God, the Eternal Father, we ask thee in the name of thy Son . . . " come out of a mouth that is clean, that does not use profanity or tell raunchy jokes or stories.

It's true. Nothing feels as good as the peace that comes with being clean. Nothing! There is no sin that feels as good as being clean. Nothing can compare with the feeling that if you were to die today, you could face the Lord with clean hands and a pure heart. That's what peace is.

Now, here's an important point to consider. Repentance is like soap. Repentance is like a hot shower that washes away all the sweat and the filth, leaving you fresh and clean. Some sins require very strong soap. But even that kind of soap is available from your bishop and from the Lord. Jesus is so powerful. Did you hear me? *Jesus is so powerful.* He can make us clean. He's the only one who can do that. No one else can bring us real peace. No one. We need Jesus. We all need him. We can't be with him again unless we're absolutely clean. We've talked about clean hands, *but there's more.*

Let's say you had to teach Sunday School one day, and you asked your class, "Why do we love Jesus?" What kind of responses would you get? Your list would probably look like this:

Because he died for us.

Because he loved us.

Because he makes it possible to return to our Father in Heaven.

Because he showed us how to live.

Because he can make us clean.

All of those answers are right. We must be made clean, because no unclean thing can enter into the kingdom of heaven, *but there's more.*

Sometimes we focus so much on the fact that Jesus can make us clean, and that he died for us, that we forget another powerful part of his wonderful atonement. It is amazing and miraculous, and we've talked a little bit about it already. Would you like to know what it is?

Remember that when I was about to give a blessing to that young woman in my ward, the scripture I thought of as I stared at my hands said, "He that hath clean hands, and a pure heart" (Psalm 24:4). Look at it closely. There's something more than just "clean hands" in that verse, isn't there? What is a "pure heart"? What exactly does that mean? Perhaps the atonement of Jesus does two things: it cleanses our hands *and* purifies our hearts. Clean hands and pure hearts are obviously not the same thing. If I'm cleansed from my sins but my heart isn't pure, then I'm just a sinner who hasn't sinned recently.[1] That's not enough! Elder Dallin H. Oaks explained it beautifully:

> A person who sins is like a tree that bends easily in the wind. On a windy and rainy day the tree bends so deeply against the ground that the leaves become soiled with mud, like sin. If we only focus on cleaning the leaves, the weakness in the tree that allowed it to bend and soil its leaves may remain. Merely cleaning the leaves does not strengthen the tree.[2]

I love that analogy. (I think it's fun that Elder *Oaks* would use a tree as an example.) If the tree is cleaned, that's nice, we have a clean tree. But what happens when another storm comes? Right. The tree gets soiled again, and again, and again! The tree must be strengthened. It must be changed. Just cleaning the tree isn't enough! Clean leaves are like clean hands, and the strengthened tree is like a purified heart.

Let's talk about hearts for a minute. I gave my brother one of my kidneys a few years back. It was a remarkable experience, a miraculous experience. For a few weeks, my whole family felt very close. It was wonderful. I wouldn't want to do it again, though. Come to think of it, I don't think it's possible to do it again. I'm fresh out of spare kidneys. Kidneys are essential equipment, but what you, and I, and everyone else needs just as critically is a new heart. We all need a "heart transplant," and through the power of the Atonement, we can get one.

When the scriptures speak about the heart, they're normally not referring to the four-chambered pump. They're referring to our inmost desires and motives, or something even deeper, like our "nature." When we talk about purifying our heart, we're not talking about being cleansed for individual sins. We're talking about changing our "sinful-ness," or our desire to sin. The brother of Jared explained it this way: "Because of the fall, our natures have become evil continually" (Ether 3:2). Do you see that? *All* of us have been affected by the Fall. We need a new heart.

Think for a moment: What would you give to be really close to God? Would you give your money? Hmmm, the Lord doesn't need your money. In fact, he doesn't need any worldly possessions. Would you give up the most worldly TV show you watch? Maybe a soap opera or two? Would you give up gossiping? Would you give up complaining or being rude to members of your family? Are there any other "favorite sins" you can think of? What is the price tag for this new heart transplant, anyway? Well, it's a high price. It's not just our favorite sins—it's all of them. It's our whole fallen nature.

A Lamanite king set a fine example of being willing to do anything to know God. His prayer is beautiful. It's interesting that one of the most inspiring prayers in all of the scriptures was offered by a Lamanite investigator:

> Oh God, Aaron hath told me that there is a God; and if there is a God, and if thou art God, wilt thou make thyself known unto me, and I will give away all my sins to know thee. (Alma 22:18)

I love that. "I'll give away all my sins." King Lamoni's father wanted to pay the price. I'll give up my old heart for a new one that has no desire to sin. Sounds like a good trade, doesn't it? Who does that heart transplant? Can you do surgery on yourself? No. But the Lord performed many heart transplants. Let's hop in our scriptural time machine and make three stops through the Book of Mormon. The purpose of our trip is to discover *who* actually performs the heart transplants.

Stop One, about 124 B.C.: Look! King Benjamin is speaking to his people:

> And they had viewed themselves in their own car-
> nal state, even less than the dust of the earth. And
> they all cried aloud with one voice, saying: O have
> mercy, and apply the atoning blood of Christ that we
> may receive forgiveness of our sins [clean hands], and
> our hearts may be purified [pure hearts]; for we
> believe in Jesus Christ, the Son of God, who created
> heaven and earth, and all things; who shall come
> down among the children of men. (Mosiah 4:2)

Stop Two, about 124 B.C.: Look! Now they're noticing their change of heart:

> And they all cried with one voice, saying: Yea, we
> believe all the words which thou hast spoken unto
> us; and also, we know of their surety and truth,
> because of the Spirit of the Lord Omnipotent, which
> has wrought a mighty change in us, or in our hearts,
> that we have no more disposition to do evil, but to
> do good continually. (Mosiah 5:2)

Stop Three, about 83 B.C.: See that? Alma the Younger is speaking of the people who were baptized by Alma the Elder:

> Behold, he [God] changed their hearts; yea, he
> awakened them out of a deep sleep [a spiritual
> snooze], and they awoke unto God. (Alma 5:7)

So how do we—you and I—receive this change of heart? How do we get to the point where the question we ask is not "How bad can I be?" but "How good can I be?" The answers are in examples 1–3 above. We *desire* to reach that point, we *work* for it, and we *pray* for it. Every day! And we have the faith that the Lord can take us there.

Please be careful that you don't get discouraged. Some people, like Paul, Enos, and King Benjamin's people, had their hearts changed in an instant. They actually lost their desire for sin in a split second. For others of us, it may take a lifetime. President Ezra Taft Benson made me feel much better when he explained:

> But we must be cautious as we discuss these remarkable examples. Though they are real and powerful, they are the exception more than the rule. For every Paul, for every Enos, and for every King Lamoni, there are hundreds and thousands of people who find the process of repentance much more subtle, much more imperceptible. Day by day they move closer to the Lord, little realizing they are building a godlike life. They live quiet lives of goodness, service, and commitment. They are like the Lamanites, who the Lord said "were baptized with fire and with the Holy Ghost, *and they knew it not."* (3 Nephi 9:20; italics added.)[3]

Every time you pray, you can ask the Lord not only to cleanse you from your sins, but to change your heart so that you can lose your desire to sin. I like to use Nephi's words when I pray: "O Lord, . . . wilt thou make me that I may shake at the appearance of sin" (2 Nephi 4:31). *Make me shake.* Isn't that great? Once again, remember that every verse in the Book of Mormon was handpicked for us in our day. I think Nephi was sharing with us the way he prayed so that we could use it too. Why else would he tell us? Here's an example of how you might use Nephi's words:

> O Lord, I'm going to school today, and in my gym class some guys always get out some bad magazines. O Lord, please make me shake! Please take away my desire to sin, please change my heart so that I have no more disposition to do evil but to do good continually. Please, Lord, make me shake at the appearance of sin!

Or how about this one:

> O Father, I have some friends who like to gossip. Sometimes it's hard to get out of it. Sometimes, in a strange way, the gossip seems to make us closer, but I know it's wrong. O Lord, please make me shake! Please change my heart. Please help me lose all my desire to sin!

Do you see what I mean? You don't have to fight temptation all by yourself. The best way to fight temptation is to do everything you can and then add God's power. Pray for a new heart, plead for it, and believe God can give it to you—every single day. We need him every hour. Unfortunately, the adversary never gives up on us, and we must never forget to pray for power to overcome.

I often hear teenagers say, "My parents don't trust me." I love it when they say that! Because I love to show them this quote from President Gordon B. Hinckley:

> I am reminded of what I heard from a man—a great, strong, and wise man—who served in the presidency of this Church years ago. His daughter was going out on a date, and her father said to her, "Be careful. Be careful of how you act and what you say."
>
> She replied, "Daddy, don't you trust me?"
>
> He responded, "I don't entirely trust myself. One never gets too old nor too high in the Church that the adversary gives up on him."[4]

And the adversary won't give up on you, either. That's why we must never give up praying for assistance.

Now we need to talk about something that is very sad. As you know, there is a dangerous attitude that is spreading like a virus among many people. It's called the "sin now, repent later" idea. If you've been listening in general conference recently, you know this is true. Listen again:

There appears to be an increasing tendency and temptation for young people to sample the forbidden things of the world, not with the intent to embrace them permanently, but with the knowing decision to indulge in them momentarily as though they held a value of some kind too important or exciting to pass by.[5]

Yes, one can repent of moral transgression. The miracle of forgiveness is real, and true repentance is accepted of the Lord. But it is not pleasing to the Lord prior to a mission, or at any time, to sow one's wild oats, to engage in sexual transgression of any nature, and then to expect that planned confession and quick repentance will satisfy the Lord.[6]

People who embrace the "sin now, repent later" idea obviously believe in Jesus, but don't love him very much. Such people believe that the Atonement can "clean our hands," but they somehow forget or absolutely ignore the "pure heart" part. A heart that asks, "How bad can I be?" is not a pure heart. A heart that has "sought to do wickedly" (see 1 Nephi 10:21) and is "procrastinating the day of repentance" (see Alma 34:34) is not clean. I'll show you what I mean.

Wherefore, if ye have sought to do wickedly [asking "how bad can I be?"] in the days of your probation, then ye are found unclean before the judgment seat of God: and no unclean thing can dwell with God; wherefore, ye must be cast off forever. (1 Nephi 10:21)

Uncleanness is not what we're after. Filthiness isn't fun. We want to be clean. I'm convinced that most of the youth reading this book really desire to be clean. I am thrilled, dazzled, and often intimidated by some of the young people I've met in this church. I recall attending a youth conference at a small university near Arkadelphia, Arkansas. Several stakes were in attendance. The youth were so excited to be there! They had never been surrounded by so many Latter-day Saints in their life! When the time for work-shops came, they sat in the front. They opened their scrip-tures and sat on the edge of their seats. They listened, they took notes, they smiled. I was a new teacher, and I was overwhelmed. I just loved them—and I knew that the Lord loved them even more.

Later, I sat in amazement and witnessed a testimony meet-ing that lasted for four hours. Young people, eager to share their feelings, were lined up on both sides of the auditorium, and the lines were still there when the meeting had to be closed. I was so overwhelmed I couldn't speak. I guess at that moment I began to understand what prophets had been saying for years: "God has saved for the final inning some of his strongest children, who will help bear off the kingdom triumphantly."[7] I was reminded of the hymn we sing, "As Zion's youth in latter days, we stand with *valiant heart*" (*Hymns,* no. 256; emphasis added). And they did.

It seemed to me that many of those young people had already received a heart transplant. Even at their young age, it seemed they had lost their desire to sin. They came to earth with the potential to be valiant, and they gave up their old heart and their desire to sin for a new heart that just wanted to be pure.

You see, repentance is a process, and repentance has steps, but it's also an attitude. Some people want to repent, but they're not *repentant*—in other words, they feel they should go through the steps of repentance because they're "post" to, or because that was part of their plan, but they haven't really been convinced of the awfulness of sin and rebellion against God. They want to repent, but they have no plans to change their attitude, at least not yet. They want clean hands, but their hearts are not yet pure.

They are confused. Somewhere, they got the idea that the choice is between repenting or not repenting. That's not the choice. The choice is "repent or suffer." And we're not talking about just any kind of suffering, but the kind Jesus endured, "which suffering caused myself, even God, the greatest of all, to tremble because of pain, and to bleed at every pore, and to suffer both body and spirit" (D&C 19:18).

When people really want to repent, they, well, really want to repent! They are more concerned with what Father in Heaven thinks than with what their friends or the world will think. The embarrassment doesn't stop them, the "what will the bishop think" doesn't stop them; they won't let anything stop them. Their hearts want to be clean and at peace, and they're willing to give whatever it takes. They, like King Lamoni's father, are willing to "give away all [their] sins to know [God]" (Alma 22:18).

It's amazing to think that there will come a day when we will stand before the Lord, face to face, and account for our lives. We will remember everything, and we will have to account for it. When I think about that day (which may be closer than we think), Alma's question becomes the most important question of all:

> I say unto you, can ye look up to God at that day with a pure heart and clean hands? I say unto you, can you look up, having the image of God engraven upon your countenances? (Alma 5:19)

Alma gives us the other option if we don't repent:

> For our words will condemn us, yea, all our works will condemn us; we shall not be found spotless; and our thoughts will also condemn us; and in this awful state we shall not dare to look up to our God; and we would fain be glad if we could command the

rocks and the mountains to fall upon us to hide us from his presence. (Alma 12:14)

Can you imagine being so ashamed that you want the mountains to fall on you to hide you? Wow. Let's take another look at that scripture and include some modern terms that show a heart that isn't pure:

> For our *profanity and gossip* will condemn us, yea, all our *deliberate sin* will condemn us; we shall not be found spotless; and our *off-color TV shows and movies* will also condemn us; and in this awful state we shall not dare to look up to our God; and we would fain be glad if we could command the rocks and the mountains to fall upon us to hide us from his presence.

Whoa, that's sobering. Alma really says it well, "In this awful state *we shall not dare* to look up." Ouch.

Sometimes I think about all the things I want. I wish I were six foot four, I wish my job paid better, I wish I had a newer car. But then I go to church, or anywhere else where the Spirit is present, and something changes inside. In those times, if you were to ask me what I want more than anything else in the world, I could tell you in five words: "I want to look up."

Well, my friend, I'm going to heaven, and I'm taking my wife with me (as soon as I find her). And I want you to be there too. There is no way I'm going to let this filthy and disgusting world stain my hands and poison my heart. Let's *all* go back, okay? Nephi was so positive when he said, "And I pray the Father in the name of Christ that many of us, *if not all*, may be saved in his kingdom at that great and last day" (2 Nephi 33:12; emphasis added). I hope that all of us—you and me, my friend—at that amazing and wonderful day can come into Jesus' presence and "look up" with clean hands and a pure heart.

Well, it's almost time for Third Period. I'll see you then.

EXTRA CREDIT

Life in Christ, Robert L. Millet (Salt Lake City: Bookcraft, 1990), especially chapter 9.

SECOND PERIOD ENDNOTES

1. See Stephen E. Robinson, *Believing Christ* (Salt Lake City: Deseret Book, 1992), pp. 27–28.
2. Dallin H. Oaks, "Sin and Suffering," Brigham Young University seventeen-stake fireside, August 5, 1990.
3. Ezra Taft Benson, in *Repentance* (Salt Lake City: Deseret Book, 1990), pp. 6–7.
4. Gordon B. Hinckley, "Trust and Accountability," Brigham Young University devotional address, October 13, 1992.
5. Dean L. Larsen, *Ensign,* May 1983, p. 35.
6. Ezra Taft Benson, *Ensign,* May 1986, pp. 44–45.
7. Ezra Taft Benson, *The Teachings of Ezra Taft Benson* (Salt Lake City: Bookcraft, 1988), p. 105.

Purity 101

How Do I Repent?

Every soul confined to a concentration camp of sin and guilt has a key to the gate. The adversary cannot hold them if they know how to use it. The key is labeled repentance.

—Boyd K. Packer

This chapter is going to be a challenge. I wonder if you would mind helping me with this one. Before I write much more, I need some input from you. I need to know if you're understanding what I'm writing. How can we do that? Hey, I have an idea! Would you like to go on a *field trip* to my computer room in Provo, Utah? Wow, such excitement! Do you think you could somehow climb through this book and come out of my computer and sit here for a second and help me write this? Go ahead, just stick your face in the book, or close your eyes and say, "Oh, Auntie Em, there's no place like home," or something. Are you ready? Go ahead, try it . . .

Wow—you did it! Are you okay? Little kink in your neck there? Oooh. Sorry about that. Here, here's a Pop Tart. Feel better? Good. Thanks for joining me. Do you like my computer room? Yeah, I know, lots of books, huh? I love books. This will be so much fun, having you sit right here! Now, if I'm explaining something and you're not getting it, just give me a confused look, okay? Great.

You see, I believe that teenagers like you who take the time to read Church books are the cream of the crop. They are wonderful. My guess is that a teenager like you is doing pretty well in keeping the commandments and everything, and might not think he or she needs to read a chapter on repentance. On the other hand, *everyone* needs to repent. And knowing what the steps are might help us . . .

Hey, did you hear that? I think the mail truck is here. Should we go outside and get the mail? I love getting the mail. Let's go. You can leave that unlocked; we're coming right back.

Wow, isn't it nice out today? It's hard to stay inside and work on the computer on a day like this, isn't it. It's lookin' like barbecue and volleyball time to me . . . is that it? Did you get it all out? Looks like mostly junk mail, huh. Let's see, sweepstakes entry, chuck that; do I need a credit card at only 9.9 percent interest? No, chuck that. Catalogs, no, I have everything I need, chuck that. My car is due for another oil change and filter, and—oh, there's a personal letter. Another Dear John, no doubt. Let's go back inside and read it. *(Yes, this is an actual letter I received.)*

Dear Brother Bytheway:

I cannot begin to tell you my failings, the list would be too long. I hate being wicked and un-Christlike. I want to be clean and Christlike. I wish I could feel comfortable talking to my bishop, but I cannot.

How can I be forgiven? How do I repent? These questions may sound stupid, but I do not know how to repent. I love my Heavenly Father and Jesus Christ with all my heart. I want to return to my eternal family so much. This Church is as true as true can be. I know the Book of Mormon is true because I have prayed about it and I know.

I have hated my life so much sometimes that I just cry and wish I was dead. I want to serve a mission, be married in the temple, and replenish the earth. I cannot do any of these things until I learn how to repent. I want to be clean and I want to feel loved every day of my life. Please, help me to repent.

Thank you for listening.

Love,

Nicole [not her real name]

I'm so proud of Nicole for asking, "How do I repent?" I wonder if she realizes how much progress she has made already. She's not resisting repentance—she wants it. It sounds like she's already working on the first step.

Let's try to answer Nicole's letter. First we'll talk about the steps of repentance, then we'll try to answer some commonly asked questions about repentance . . . what's that? You say you brought some commonly asked questions with you? Oh, good! Hey, you know, you're kind of representing everybody who's out there reading this book. Kind of a "field trip by proxy." That's great. Hand me any of those questions as we go along, okay?

First off, could you reach over and grab that little paperback book, *Faith Precedes the Miracle,* by Spencer W. Kimball? It has a wonderful explanation of the steps of repentance. Let's turn to page 180:

> Repentance could well fall into five steps:
> 1. Conviction of and sorrow for sin
> 2. Abandonment of sin
> 3. Confession of sin
> 4. Restitution for sin
> 5. Doing the will of the Lord

President Kimball goes into more depth, but let's stop here for a minute. I have a feeling that many people, adults and teens alike, stop right there and think that the "steps of repentance" *are* repentance. They're not! The steps are just the tip of the iceberg. Have you heard that expression before? The tip of the iceberg, the visible part, is *not* the iceberg—it's evidence that there's something much larger beneath the surface. In the same way, the steps of repentance by themselves are not repentance. A superficial run-through of those steps is not repentance. True repentance is a deep, involved process. When someone is truly repenting, yes, they *will* go through the steps of repentance, but those steps are merely the visible evidence that something much larger is going on beneath the surface.

And what is that "something much larger" going on beneath the surface? Well, to use the words we've already used in this book, it's the heart transplant, the "change of heart." It's going from the "How-bad-can-I-be" attitude, or the "How-good-am-I-post-to-be" attitude, to the "I-want-to-be-valiant" attitude. It's when we begin to love righteousness more than sin.

Now, back to the steps of repentance. Elder Theodore M. Burton said this:

> Many times a bishop will write: "I feel he has suffered enough!" But suffering is not repentance. Suffering comes from *lack* of complete repentance. A stake president will write: "I feel he has been punished enough!" But punishment is not repentance. Punishment *follows* disobedience and *precedes* repentance. A husband will write: "My wife has confessed everything!" But confession is not repentance. Confession is an admission of guilt that occurs *as* repentance begins. A wife will write: "My husband is filled with remorse!" But remorse is not repentance. Remorse and sorrow continue because a person has *not* yet fully repented. But if suffering, punishment, confession, remorse, and sorrow are not repentance, what *is* repentance?[1]

Good question. *What is repentance?* Here, have another Pop Tart, and let's go back to President Kimball. He said that the first step of repentance is conviction of and sorrow for sin.

1. CONVICTION OF AND SORROW FOR SIN

That doesn't mean just saying, "Oh, I'm supposed to be sorry? Oh, okay. I'm sorry." It's a little more involved than that. Go ahead and read President Kimball's explanation:

> To be sorry for our sin, we must know something of its serious implications. . . . We are sorry. We are willing to make amends, pay penalties, to suffer excommunication, if necessary. . . .
>
> If one is sorry only because his sin was uncovered, his repentance is not complete. Godly sorrow causes one to harness desire and to determine to do right regardless of consequences; this kind of sorrow brings righteousness and will work toward forgiveness. (Page 180)

That's what it means to really be sorry. You'd be willing to do anything needed to get things cleared up. Yes, even seeing the bishop. Some people carry around serious burdens and regrets for years because they're too embarrassed to talk with their bishop. They are worried that their parents or friends will find out, and I guess that's understandable. But if we're more worried about what our peers think than what the Lord thinks, we're not truly sorry. When we are filled with godly sorrow, we will be willing to do *anything* the Lord requires.

So, guilt can be good! My car has a little warning light that says, "Service Engine Soon." Some maintenance on my car I can do myself, but other things require outside help. Sorrow and guilt are like a little warning light telling us there's something wrong that needs to be fixed. And, as with my car, some repairs we can't do by ourselves. We'll talk more about that when we get to confession. Just remember, *acting* sorry is not the same as *being* sorry. Okay, let's go back to President Kimball and talk about the second step:

2. ABANDONMENT OF SIN

> One discontinues his error when he has a full realization of the gravity of his sin and when he is willing to comply with the laws of God. The thief may abandon his evil in prison, but true repentance would have

him forsake it before his arrest and return his booty
without enforcement. The sex offender as well as any
other transgressor who voluntarily ceases his unholy
practices is headed toward forgiveness. (Page 180)

Let's look at that last phrase again: "any . . . transgressor
who voluntarily ceases his unholy practices is headed
toward forgiveness." President Kimball touches on two
important concepts there. First, if you go voluntarily to confess, it's much better than if you had no intention of
confessing and you just got caught. The second idea is that a
person who ceases sinning "is headed toward forgiveness."
In other words, repentance isn't over yet, but the person is
on the path.

Let me explain with a little math problem. You see—
uh-oh, you've got that confused look. What does math have
to do with abandoning a sin? You'll see what I'm doing in a
minute. Let's say you have a math problem. You're supposed
to take a number, and add and subtract some other numbers. We'll start with the number 5. Now watch this carefully,
okay?

Start with five: 5
1. Now add twelve to it: $5 + 12 = 17$
2. Subtract four from it: $17 - 4 = 13$
3. Add six to it: $13 + 6 = 18$
4. Subtract five from it: $18 - 5 = 13$
5. Add ten to it: $13 + 10 = 23$
6. Now subtract four from it: $23 - 4 = 19$
7. Add ten to it: $19 + 10 = 29$

Have you noticed anything? Look closely. Right! We made
a mistake back there on step 3. Thirteen plus six equals
nineteen, not eighteen. We can continue with step 4 and
keep going as long as we want to, adding and subtracting
more numbers, but it won't come out right, because we
made a mistake on step 3.

The point is, some people believe that if they simply stop

doing the sin, that's repentance. "Well, I haven't done that for a long time, so I'm probably forgiven." It doesn't work that way. You have to go back and correct the mistake. Like in our math problem, if you *don't* go back and correct the mistake, you'll never come out right in the end. Forsaking the sin is not enough. You have to completely correct it by repentance. Get it?

It *is* important to forsake our sins, though. The Lord said, "Go your ways and sin no more; but unto that soul who sinneth shall the former sins return" (D&C 82:7).

That idea scares a lot of people. They don't want to sin anymore, but they're afraid that they might, somewhere down the road. This is one of those instances where I believe the Lord looks on our hearts. He knows we can't become perfect overnight. But if we're fully committed in our heart not to sin again, I believe the Lord accepts that kind of repentance. On the other hand, if our heart is saying, "I just want to get through these steps and see what happens," then perhaps we're not really sorry.

What's that? Oh, good, you have a question from one of your classmates. Let's read it:

> *The part about forsaking the sin and never doing it again always scares me. For example, if I get mad at my sister, and I repent, how can I know I will never get mad at her again? How can I be sure? It makes it so I don't want to repent because I can't promise it won't happen again.*

Hmmm, that's an excellent question. I think we can answer it from the scriptures. In Mosiah 26:30, the Lord told Alma, "Yea, and as often as my people repent will I forgive them their trespasses against me." Let's read that again slowly: *"As often as my people repent will I forgive them their trespasses against me."*

Does this seem a little confusing? On the one hand we're

saying, "If you sin and repent, you can't do it again," and on the other hand we're saying, "but if you do, you can repent." I have had this question myself, but I found the answer in my *Book of Mormon Student Manual*. Let's read what it says about Mosiah 26:30:

> How Long-suffering Is the Lord?
>
> Even though a mighty change occurs at rebirth, no one becomes perfect overnight. So the principle of repentance is needed as one endeavors to go on unto perfection (Hebrews 6:1) and as he endures to the end. *Satan would have him believe that, once forgiven, any misstep is fatal and irreparable.* But this passage shows that Satan is a liar. *Every young person should have this passage memorized as a source of hope.* But he should understand that it is not a license to commit willful sin or try to take unrighteous advantage of the Lord's mercy, for the Lord has also said, "but unto that soul who sinneth shall the former sins return." (D&C 82:7.) Though at first these two scriptures (Mosiah 26:30; D&C 82:7) may seem contradictory, together they teach the true mercy and justice of the Lord.[2]

Does that help? So you repent with all your heart, and you don't plan on repeating that sin. But if you do, you start the repentance process again. The main question becomes, what's in your heart? Did you approach it with a lazy, "I'll-probably-do-it-again" attitude, or was it a serious, "I'm-really-going-to-try-to-forsake-that-sin" attitude? The Lord doesn't require you to be perfect right now, but he wants you to be trying. Make sense? Okay, step three from President Kimball:

3. CONFESSION OF SIN

> The confession of sin is an important element in repentance. Many offenders have seemed to feel that a few prayers to the Lord were sufficient and they

have thus justified themselves in hiding their sins. The Proverbs tell us:

"He that covereth his sins shall not prosper: but whoso confesseth and forsaketh them shall have mercy." (Proverbs 28:13.)

"By this ye may know if a man repenteth of his sins—behold, he will confess them and forsake them." (D&C 58:43.)

Especially grave errors such as sexual sins shall be confessed to the bishop as well as to the Lord. There are two remissions that one might wish to have: first, the forgiveness from the Lord, and second, the forgiveness of the Lord's church through its leaders. (Page 181)

Okay, let's talk for a minute. All sins, great or small, must be confessed to the Lord. As you've probably already figured out, the Lord knows what your sins are. You're not going to surprise him or tell him anything new. But you still need to acknowledge to the Lord that you have sinned. You also need to confess to anyone you may have hurt or injured because of your sin. And, as President Kimball mentioned, especially serious sins need to be confessed to the bishop. Why? Well, the Lord said to Alma, "If he confess his sins before thee and me, and repenteth in the sincerity of his heart, him shall ye forgive, and I will forgive him also" (Mosiah 26:29).

Why does the bishop have to be involved? The simple answer is that the bishop can help guide you through the repentance process. But there's more; let's take another look at my excellent *Book of Mormon Student Manual:*

When a member's sins have been discovered by or reported to Church leaders, they are duty bound to take action for three reasons: [1] to preserve the good name of the Church [to show the world that it does not condone sin], [2] to help the sinner, [3] and to assure the righteous that Church leaders are not trying to hide or overlook the sins of some while punishing the sins of others. A confession of guilt is required on these occasions as part of the proof of repentance.[3]

In case you're still not sure why the bishop needs to be involved, I'll put it another way. One time I had a persistent sore throat. I tried everything to get rid of it: gargling, lozenges, plenty of liquids, throat sprays, everything! But it wouldn't go away. Finally I got smart and went to the doctor. He had medicine that I couldn't get on my own. Did you hear that with your spiritual ears? *He had medicine that I couldn't get on my own*, and he had authority to get that medicine for me. Can you imagine me saying, "Well, I'd like to get rid of this sore throat but I just can't go see a doctor." Think of it this way: saying, "I can't go see the bishop, I'm too ashamed!" is like saying, "I can't go see the doctor, I'm too sick!"

Of course, anyone grappling with major sins may feel reluctant to confess to the bishop. But everyone I know who has actually followed through, confessed to the bishop, and repented has said that although it was difficult, it was a wonderful and positive experience. And they always came out of the bishop's office rejoicing, feeling renewed gratitude for the Atonement, and feeling like a tremendous load had been taken from their shoulders. Most of them say, "I wish I had gone sooner." And so does the Lord. He invites us to repent, to procrastinate no more, and says, in effect, "Put the weight on my shoulders."

Oh good, here's another question from out there in reading land:

Exactly what sins have to be confessed to the bishop?

Good question. As a rule of thumb, if you think a sin is

serious but you're not sure if you should talk to the bishop, talk to the bishop. In another book, *The Miracle of Forgiveness,* President Kimball gave a fairly specific list:

> The confession of . . . major sins to a proper Church authority is one of those requirements made by the Lord. These sins include adultery, fornication, other sexual transgressions, and sins of comparable seriousness.[4]

As you can see, for the most part, the sins involving sexual purity are the ones that need to be confessed to the bishop. Oh, here's another comment from the class:

> *I feel like I need to talk to my bishop, but I'm too embarrassed. He's my relative, and I'm afraid my whole family and everyone else will find out.*

These are some of the toughest issues to deal with, and the answers may sound harsh, but they are true and crystal clear. First of all, the bishop is under a sacred obligation to keep confessions confidential, and to discuss them only with those who were directly involved. (Now, I know we've all heard horror stories, but if those stories are true, they are the exception and not the rule.) If your personal situation makes you feel that it is not possible for you to go to your bishop, then make an appointment with the stake president and clear things up. Don't procrastinate and stew and figure out all the worst things that could happen. The worst has already happened, and now it's time to seek forgiveness and put it behind you.

And about the embarrassment thing—you can have a little embarrassment now or a lot of embarrassment later. Brace yourself; this is harsh, but it's the way things are.

> And the rebellious shall be pierced with much sorrow; for their iniquities shall be spoken upon the

housetops, and their secret acts shall be revealed.
(D&C 1:3)

And those who are not pure, and have said they
were pure, shall be destroyed, saith the Lord God.
(D&C 132:52)

If you need to repent, this is no time to try to hide your
sins. It won't work. It's the height of foolishness to think you
can hide your sins from God. If you really want repentance,
if you really want to feel clean, no amount of anticipated
embarrassment will keep you from the bishop's office. And
once you are there, tell him everything! Elder Vaughn J.
Featherstone has said:

> A bishop may be deceived, but the Holy Ghost
> cannot. . . . What a tragedy when someone finally
> gets enough courage to go to the bishop and then
> leaves his office having only partially confessed.[5]

President Kimball continues:

> The bishop may be one's best earthly friend. He will
> hear the problems, judge the seriousness thereof,
> determine the degree of adjustment, and decide if it
> warrants an eventual forgiveness. He does this as the
> earthly representative of God, who is the master physi-
> cian, the master psychologist, the master psychiatrist.
> If repentance is sufficient, he may waive penalties,
> which is tantamount to forgiveness so far as the church
> organization is concerned. The bishop claims no
> authority to absolve sins, but he does share the bur-
> den, waive penalties, relieve tension and strain, and he
> may assure a continuation of church activity. He will
> keep the whole matter most confidential. (Page 182)

4. RESTITUTION FOR SIN

You probably already know what *restitution* means;
another word for it might be *restoration*. When we repent,

we try to "restore" what was taken away. Let's continue reading from *Faith Precedes the Miracle:*

> When one is humble in sorrow, has uncondition-
> ally abandoned the evil, and confesses to those
> assigned by the Lord, he should next restore insofar
> as possible that which was damaged. If he burglar-
> ized, he should return to the rightful owner that
> which was stolen. Perhaps one reason murder is
> unforgivable is that having taken a life, the murderer
> cannot restore it. Restitution in full is not always pos-
> sible. Virginity is impossible to give back.
>
> However, the truly repentant soul will usually find
> things that can be done to restore to some extent.
> The true spirit of repentance demands this. Ezekiel
> taught:
>
> If the wicked . . . give again that he had robbed,
> walk in the statutes of life, without committing iniq-
> uity; he shall surely live. . . . (Ezekiel 33:15.) . . .
>
> A pleading sinner must also forgive all people of
> all offenses committed against himself. The Lord is
> under no obligation to forgive us unless our hearts
> are fully purged of all hate, bitterness, and accusa-
> tions against others. (Pages 182–83)

You may have wondered why adultery is a sin next to
murder. When you think about restitution, it may help you
answer the question. A murderer cannot restore life, and one
who commits a sexual sin cannot restore purity. But the
Lord, because of his mercy, still allows a way to make restitution from the serious sin of unchastity through the wonderful and powerful doctrine of repentance. Much of that
restitution comes from the next step.

After all we've talked about, it may seem like the most difficult part of repentance is over. It isn't. Confession takes real

courage, but the hardest part is yet to come. President Kimball continues with step five:

5. DO THE WILL OF THE FATHER

The Lord in his preface to modern revelations gave us the fifth and one of the most difficult requirements to forgiveness. He says:

"For I the Lord cannot look upon sin with the least degree of allowance; Nevertheless, he that repents *and does the commandments of the Lord* shall be forgiven." (D&C 1:31-32; emphasis added.)

Under the humiliation of a guilty conscience, with the possibility of detection and consequent scandal and shame, with a striving spirit urging toward adjustment, the first steps of sorrow, abandonment, confession, and restitution must now be followed by the never-ending requirement of doing the commandments. Obviously this can hardly be done in a day, a week, a month, or a year. This is an effort extending through the balance of life. (Page 183)

So there's the toughest part: Do the will of the Father, and live the gospel from now on! It reminds me of Jesus' words to the woman taken in adultery: "Go, and sin no more" (John 8:11).

We've managed to cover the five steps of repentance outlined by President Kimball. Does it all make sense? It's a sobering subject, isn't it. It would be a lot simpler to just avoid sinning. I like President Ezra Taft Benson's comment, "It is better to prepare and prevent, than repair and repent."

Let's take some more questions from the field-trip group:

How do you know when you're forgiven? How long does it take?

Well, that's a good one. As you know, we live in a world of drive-through dining, instant cocoa, and microwave dinners. We want everything right now! But there are a few things that cannot be rushed, that will always take time. How much time? With repentance, it's not possible to give a blanket answer. We cannot dictate our timetable to the Lord. He will answer our prayers in his own way and in his own time, but we have a few hints from the scriptures. Enos prayed all day and into the night to receive forgiveness of his sins. And Alma the Younger, in one of the most wonderful stories of repentance ever told, said that he was "racked . . . with the pains of a damned soul" for three days and three nights before he received forgiveness (Alma 36:16).

Elder Henry B. Eyring told of a young man who had gone through deep and painful repentance. This young man was scheduled to be married in the temple, but he wanted to know he was forgiven. He wanted to be the best he could be for his new bride. He asked Elder Eyring, who was his bishop at that time, how he could be *sure* the Lord had forgiven him. Bishop Eyring said he would try to find out. A few days later, the bishop was in the company of then Elder Spencer W. Kimball (whom we've quoted so much in this chapter). He explained the situation, and asked:

> "How can he get that revelation? How can he know whether his sins are remitted?"
>
> I thought Elder Kimball would talk to me about fasting or prayer or listening for the still small voice. But he surprised me. Instead he said, "Tell me something about the young man."
>
> I said, "What would you like to know?"
>
> And then he began a series of the most simple questions. Some of the ones I remember were:
>
> "Does he come to his priesthood meetings?"
>
> I said, after a moment's thought, "Yes."
>
> "Does he come early?"
>
> "Yes."
>
> "Does he sit down front?"

I thought for a moment and then realized, to my amazement, that he did.

"Does he home teach?"

"Yes."

"Does he go early in the month?"

"Yes, he does."

"Does he go more than once?"

"Yes."

I can't remember the other questions. But they were all like that—little things, simple acts of obedience, of submission. And for each question I was surprised that my answer was always yes. Yes, he wasn't just at all his meetings: he was early; he was smiling; he was there not only with his whole heart, but the broken heart of a little child, as he was every time the Lord asked anything of him. And after I had said yes to each of his questions, Elder Kimball looked at me, paused, and then very quietly said, "There is your revelation."[6]

Isn't that an interesting story? I love it. But let's be careful. Is Elder Eyring saying that all you have to do to be forgiven is go early to meetings and smile a lot? Of course not! This is a perfect example of the "tip-of-the-iceberg" concept we talked about earlier. The simple acts of obedience by this young man were evidence that something much larger was going on beneath the surface. His heart was changed. He wanted to be valiant! He wouldn't *think* of asking, "How bad can I be?" He wanted to be the best he could be.

If you want to learn more about repentance, go to the Book of Mormon. Alma teaches us so much about repentance in Alma 36. For example, we know that the Lord will not remember our sins when we sincerely repent: "Behold, he who has repented of his sins, the same is forgiven, and I, the Lord, remember them no more" (D&C 58:42). But what about us? Do *we* remember them? Let's read from Alma:

> Now, as my mind caught hold upon this thought, I cried within my heart: O Jesus, thou Son of God, have mercy on me, who am in the gall of bitterness, and am encircled about by the everlasting chains of death.
>
> And now, behold, when I thought this, *I could remember my pains no more;* yea, I was harrowed up by the memory of my sins no more.
>
> And oh, what joy, and what marvelous light I did behold; yea, my soul was filled with joy as exceeding as was my pain! (Alma 36:18–20; emphasis added)

It sounds to me as if we will *remember* our sins, but the memory of them will not cause us *pain* anymore! Perhaps this is another way we can know we are forgiven. We'll remember our sins, but we will know we have sincerely repented and put them behind us. We won't be "harrowed up" by their memory anymore.

In another place in the Book of Mormon, we read that King Benjamin's people knew they were forgiven because they felt peace:

> And it came to pass that after they had spoken these words the Spirit of the Lord came upon them, and they were filled with joy, having received a remission of their sins, and having *peace of conscience*, because of the exceeding faith which they had in Jesus Christ who should come. (Mosiah 4:3; emphasis added)

A young friend of mine wrote, "I hope that through all I have experienced I may be able to influence others to steer clear of sin. It is not a happy path. It may seem fun, but one mistake leads to others, and it's just a slippery slide that ends in the mud, and it's so hard to climb out."

She's right. Sin is like mud. Elder Richard G. Scott gave a very beautiful and tender talk called "We Love You—Please Come Back." He talked about mud too, and how we should deal with our memories of past mistakes:

> If you, through poor judgment, were to cover your shoes with mud, would you leave them that way? Of course not. You would cleanse and restore them. Would you then gather the residue of mud and place it in an envelope to show others the mistake that you made? No. Neither should you continue to relive forgiven sin. Every time such thoughts come into your mind, turn your heart in gratitude to the Savior, who gave His life that we, through faith in Him and obedience to His teachings, can overcome transgression and conquer its depressing influence in our lives.[7]

Nine years later, Elder Scott gave another beautiful talk about repentance. He used President Kimball's five steps and then added a sixth:

6. RECOGNITION OF THE SAVIOR

> Of all the necessary steps to repentance, I testify that the most critically important is for you to have a conviction that forgiveness comes because of the Redeemer.[8]

As you grow older, you will find that you become more and more sensitive to the fact that sin separates you from God. And because of this, you'll become more and more grateful for Jesus Christ, and for his power to rescue us, and help us, and cleanse us. I am comforted by the words of one of my most honored and respected heroes, Nephi. He was amazing to me. Someone once said, "The closer we get to

God, the further away we'll realize we really are," and I think of that whenever I read Nephi's lament:

> O wretched man that I am! Yea, my heart sor-roweth because of my flesh; my soul grieveth because of mine iniquities.
>
> I am encompassed about, because of the tempta-tions and the sins which do so easily beset me.
>
> And when I desire to rejoice, my heart groaneth because of my sins; nevertheless, I know in whom I have trusted.
>
> My God hath been my support. (2 Nephi 4:17–20)

There's that last step. We must focus on Jesus, and when we do, our love for him will grow, because we will always remember him and what he has done for us to make us clean.

Wow, this has been a long one. Any more questions?

> *Sometimes when I read or hear stories about repen-tance, it sounds so hard. I want to know how willing God is to forgive us.*

God does not want anyone to suffer. He wants us to repent. Jesus has already suffered for us if we repent. There are so many scriptures I could show you to answer this question, but none better than Luke 15, the story of the prodigal son. Read this carefully, and you'll be able to see for yourself how willing Heavenly Father is to take us back from sin when we repent:

> And he said, A certain man had two sons:
>
> And the younger of them said to his father, Father, give me the portion of goods that falleth to me. And he divided unto them his living.
>
> And not many days after the younger son gathered all together, and took his journey into a far country, and there wasted his substance with riotous living.

Sorry to interrupt, but what does "riotous living" mean? Right. He was living a sinful life. Okay, keep going.

> And when he had spent all, there arose a mighty famine in that land; and he began to be in want.
>
> And he went and joined himself to a citizen of that country; and he sent him into his fields to feed swine.
>
> And he would fain have filled his belly with the husks that the swine did eat: and no man gave unto him.
>
> And when he came to himself, he said, How many hired servants of my father's have bread enough and to spare, and I perish with hunger!

Isn't that a great phrase: "He came to himself"! In other words, he figured out how empty and hollow and wrong his life had been; he realized the happiness of righteousness and honor and loyalty and family. Okay, back to the story . . .

> I will arise and go to my father, and will say unto him, Father, I have sinned against heaven, and before thee,
>
> And am no more worthy to be called thy son: make me as one of thy hired servants.
>
> And he arose, and came to his father. But when he was yet a great way off, his father saw him, and had compassion, and ran, and fell on his neck, and kissed him.

Are you listening? "When he was yet *a great way off*, his father saw him." Remember that, okay?

> And the son said unto him, Father, I have sinned against heaven, and in thy sight, and am no more worthy to be called thy son.
>
> But the father said to his servants, Bring forth the best robe, and put it on him; and put a ring on his hand, and shoes on his feet:

And bring hither the fatted calf, and kill it; and let us eat, and be merry:

For this my son was dead, and is alive again; he was lost, and is found. And they began to be merry. (Luke 15:11–24)

What does all this mean? To begin with, obviously the father in this story represents our Father in Heaven. Now, I have a question for you. You remember that the prodigal son's father saw him when he was "yet a great way off." So, where was his father? Was he in the house, doing something else, not caring about whether his child ever returned? No, no. His father was *looking for him,* searching the horizon, waiting, watching, and wondering, "Will he ever come back?" And one day, the son turned around and began the journey home. And as soon as his father saw him, he *ran.* He didn't stay on the porch and wait for his son to walk all the way back, and he didn't just walk out to meet him. He ran! Then, together, they walked home. Do you see what is being taught here?

How willing is our Father to forgive us? He is so willing that when we "arise, and come to our Father," he will run out to help us come back. Is our repentance finished? Not at all. But once our Father in Heaven sees that we have turned around and are heading home, he will run out to be with us to help us through each of the steps of repentance. What love he must have for us, to run to us and bring us home!

Well, I hope we answered Nicole's questions—and maybe some of yours, too. Just remember that repentance isn't just some steps. Real repentance is hard. It hurts. As President Kimball once said, "If a person hasn't suffered, he hasn't repented. . . . The Savior can do almost anything in the world, but he can't forgive somebody who hasn't repented."⁹ Wow.

Did you just hear something outside? It sounds like the mail truck is here again. That's unusual. Twice in one day? Oh, well, I guess it's not any more unusual than you climbing through your book and going on a field trip with the author, huh? What a strange book this is. Well, let's go get the mail.

Oh, look, it's another letter from Nicole, and it was written several months after the first one. Maybe we were in some kind of time warp when we were writing. Go ahead and read it. What does she say? *(Yes, this really is a second letter from the same young woman.)*

> Dear John:
> . . . As I said before, I was having a lot of problems with my life. I loved the Lord but I was not happy. I had sinned and I felt like just asking for forgiveness was not enough. I had to do more. I got a lot of strength and help from my seminary teacher. He suggested I talk to my bishop. When I told him my feelings, he called my bishop and arranged an appointment. From there, there was no backing down. I wanted it bad enough that I wouldn't back down either.
> My bishop was very understanding. . . . Since then, my bishop has become a dear friend I can go to in times of need. I really did feel good afterwards. I believe now that he has the true healing power of God. . . .
> Your sister in the gospel,
> Nicole

Isn't that great? She followed through and now she is so much happier. It reminds me of a scripture: "Likewise I say unto you, there is joy in the presence of the angels of God over one sinner who repenteth" (JST, Luke 15:10).

I guess that's a nice way to end Third Period. The older I get, the more I realize how much I really need the principle of repentance. I am grateful to President Spencer W. Kimball who wrote so much about repentance so that we could all understand. And most of all, I am grateful for the Savior, who suffered in Gethsemane and on Golgotha, and took all of our pains, sicknesses, transgressions, and sins upon himself, so that we could repent and change and be clean, and be able to "look up" to him again someday.

Well, I guess our field trip is over. See if you can figure out how to climb back through that book. Thanks for coming! And I'll see you in Fourth Period.

EXTRA CREDIT

Faith Precedes the Miracle, Spencer W. Kimball (Salt Lake City: Deseret Book, 1972).

The Miracle of Forgiveness, Spencer W. Kimball (Salt Lake City: Bookcraft, 1969).

"Finding Forgiveness," Richard G. Scott, *Ensign,* May 1995, pp. 75–77.

Believing Christ, Stephen E. Robinson (Salt Lake City: Deseret Book, 1992).

Within Reach, Robert L. Millet (Salt Lake City: Deseret Book, 1995).

THIRD PERIOD ENDNOTES

Division page quotation: Boyd K. Packer, *Ensign,* May 1992, p. 68.

1. Theodore M. Burton, in *Repentance* (Salt Lake City: Deseret Book, 1990), pp. 10–11.

2. *Book of Mormon Student Manual, Religion 121–122* (Salt Lake City: The Church of Jesus Christ of Latter-day Saints, 1979) p. 201; emphasis added.

3. Ibid, p. 201.

4. Spencer W. Kimball, *The Miracle of Forgiveness* (Salt Lake City: Bookcraft, 1969), p. 179.

5. Vaughn J. Featherstone, in *Repentance,* p. 58.

6. Henry B. Eyring, "Come Unto Christ," Brigham Young University seventeen-stake fireside, October 29, 1989.

7. Richard G. Scott, *Ensign,* May 1986, p. 12.

8. Richard G. Scott, *Ensign,* May 1995, p. 76.

9. *Teachings of Spencer W. Kimball,* Edward L. Kimball, ed. (Salt Lake City: Bookcraft, 1981), p. 99.

Lunch Break

A Visit to Zarahemla Burger

Well, we covered some pretty heavy subjects in the last three classes, so I think you deserve a break today. Whaddaya say we go get some lunch? Do you like fast food? Good—I'll drive.

"Hi, Honda, I'm home!" Hop in, it's unlocked. So, do you like my car? What's that you say: It's so clean? Well, my father looked at me one day with that "you'd-better-listen-up-because-this-is-profound" look and said, "A clean car is a happy car." Of course, I was deeply touched, and my life was changed forever.

So, where do you want to go? Do you want me to choose? Okay. As you've probably guessed, this is no ordinary lunch break. In fact, when we're done, you may feel as if you didn't eat a thing. But because this is no ordinary lunch break, we can do some out-of-the-ordinary things. You see, we're sitting in an imaginary Honda, but we're also in the middle of a book. It's kind of an off-the-wall book, yes, but it's still a book. Remember in the Orientation, where we learned that books are like mini time machines? Well, it's true. We can go anywhere (or should I say any*when*) we want to.

We can even go get fast food in 90 B.C. if you want. Do you believe me? Push in that lighter thingy, close your eyes, and think, "Ancient America, 90 B.C." When it pops out, we'll be there. (In the meantime, imagine a harp playing "going-back-in-time" music.) Click . . . POP!

Okay, open your eyes. (How did you read this with your eyes closed?) We made it! What do you think? Pretty weird, huh? Oh, wait, I forgot something. We have to talk a little differently, okay? Let's see, I gotta get in the mood here. . . . Behold, I see the place of feeding, and it is exceedingly close. Yea, it is called Zarahemla Burger. Behold, I will pull into the drive-up window, near the speaker, and we will place our order.

Behold, welcome to Zarahemla Burger. May I take your order, please?

Yes—I mean, Yea, we are exceedingly hungry. I'll have an Ammon Cheese, a cold Laman-ade, and an order of Nephries. But behold, this is not all. My friend has to order too. Canst thou wait whilst my friend decides?

Behold, I will wait even until thy friend orders. Just speak when ready, and I will record all thy words, and will give thee thy price.

Well, what dost thou desire? It's hard to read that reformed Egyptian menu, isn't it? I'll ask her for some help.
Behold, canst thou tell me all that thy restaurant offers?

Behold, we have many selections from the Nephi's Broken Bow[1] Vegetarian Section. Thou mayest start with a Sariah Salad . . .

Dost thou have dressing with that?

Yea, we have Rameumptom[2] Ranch, Hagoth[3] Thousand Island, and Gadianton[4] dressing.

Gadianton dressing—what's in that?

I cannot tell thee; it is a secret combination.

Oh, okay. Dost thou still have lamb chops?

Nay, for behold, all of our sheep have been chased away from the waters of Sebus.[5] But behold, Ammon is out gathering the flocks to the place of water. Soon we will have leg of lamb again. (Apparently, we will also have Arm of Bandit, but I doubt that will be on the menu.)

Wow—uh—okay, canst thou describe the Brother of Jared Burrito?

Yea, it is peaked at the ends, and tight like unto a dish.[6]

What about the Promised Land Breakfast?

Yea, it is just flowing with milk and honey.[7]

And what's the Brass Plate Special?

Behold, it is exceedingly good. People have come back two hundred miles to get it.[8]

I think we'll just have another Ammon Cheese, with a Laman-ade and Nephries.

Wouldst thou like that in our Ish-meal combo? Behold, it is cheaper that way.

Yea, that is acceptable. Behold, what are thy drink sizes? For verily we have traveled far.

We have small, medium, large, and our 32-ounce Waters of Mormon.[9] *Surely it will quench thy thirst.*

Behold, I believe all thy words, but please don't call me Shirley. We'll have two Waters-of-Mormon Laman-ades. Wilt thou accept a check?

Yea: cash, checks, and the Amaron[10] *Express card.*

Behold, that sounds good. Thank thee.

Please pull forward, and it will come to pass that I will give thee thy total at the place of payment. . . Behold, the total comes to one senum.[11]

One senum, okay, here you go—I mean, um, here thou goest.

*Behold, here is thy food, and here is thy change—a
shiblum and a leah. Have a nice day, and may it
come to pass that we will see thee again at Zarahemla
Burger.*

Thou wilt. Thank thee and farewell!

Hey, that was fun. Let's park the car and go sit at the table
underneath that tree. Our visit to Zarahemla Burger wouldn't
be complete unless we play the games they print on these
bags. It looks like you got the "exceedingly simple" games,
and I got the "exceedingly challenging" games. Let's try
yours first:

Exceedingly *Simple* Game #1

There is a cleverly hidden message inside this
baffling word puzzle! See if you can find it!
(Time limit: 20 minutes.)

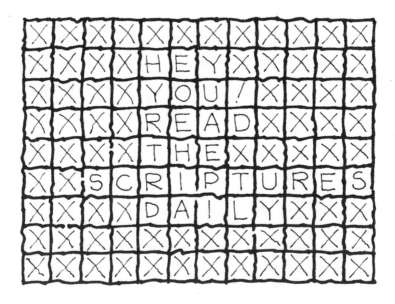

Exceedingly *Simple* Game #2

OPTICAL ILLUSION!
See if you can tell which object is bigger!
(Time limit: 5 minutes.)

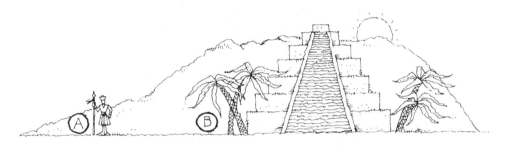

Answer: B

Exceedingly *Challenging* Game #1

There are six women mentioned by name in
the Book of Mormon: Who are they?

1. _____ (Hint: She was the first woman—1 Nephi 5:11)

2. _____ (Hint: She had several sons, including Sam, Jacob, and
Joseph—1 Nephi 8:14; 1 Nephi 18:19)

3. _____ (Hint: She and Joseph journeyed to Bethlehem—Mosiah
3:8)

4. _____ (Hint: She saw Ammon and King Lamoni unconscious—
Alma 19:16)

5. _____ (Hint: Corianton was scolded about her by his father—
Alma 39:3)

6. _____ (Hint: She was Isaac's mother—2 Nephi 8:2)

Exceedingly *Challenging* Game #2

AMMON AND KING LAMONI
Crossword Puzzle

1. Alma 17:25 Ammon did not immediately announce that he was a missionary. Instead, he offered to be a _____ to King Lamoni.

2. Alma 17:26 The flocks drank at the water of _____.

3. Alma 17:29 Ammon wanted to win the _____ of his fellow servants so that they would believe on his words.

4. Alma 17:35 The Lord promised _____ that Ammon would not be harmed.

5. Alma 17:37 Ammon withstood the blows of those who came to scatter the flocks, and they began to be _____.

6. Alma 18:2 The king thought Ammon might be the _____ Spirit.

7. Alma 18:9 While the servants were explaining to the king what had happened at the watering place, Ammon was feeding the king's _____.

8. Alma 18:23 The king told Ammon he would believe all his _____.

9. Alma 18:39 Alma taught the king the gospel, including the plan of salvation, or in other words, the plan of _____.

Note: Completing this crossword puzzle does not count as your daily scripture reading.

So, did you enjoy the games? Did you like your Laman-ade? Ah yes, the only drink that rebels when you try to swallow it. Next time we'll try the Lemuel-lime, "the beverage with an attitude." But now I think it's time to get back to class. 'Bye, Zarahemla Burger! Push the lighter thingy in again, close your eyes, and think "Back to Fourth Period."

Click . . . POP! Here we are, back to the real world. We'll visit our imagination again before this day (this book, I mean) is over. I'll see you back in class!

LUNCH BREAK ENDNOTES

1. 1 Nephi 16:18. (Wow, comedy with footnotes! What a ground-breaking book!)
2. Alma 31:21.
3. Alma 63:5.
4. Helaman 3:23.
5. Alma 18:7.
6. Ether 2:17.
7. Doctrine and Covenants 38:18.
8. 1 Nephi 3:24.
9. Mosiah 18:30.
10. Omni 1:4.
11. Alma 11:3.

Listening Skills 101

Recognizing the Spirit

God does not send thunder if a still, small voice is enough.

—Neal A. Maxwell

Have you ever felt like a spiritual amoeba? Have you ever said, "How come I never have any spiritual experiences?" Perhaps you've wondered if you've ever really "felt the Spirit" at all. Well, my guess is that you've had many spiritual experiences—you just haven't recognized them as such. I hope Fourth Period will help.

I remember a very interesting poster I saw a few years ago. It was a drawing of an old man dancing around some train tracks holding a small radio near his ear. Underneath the picture it read: "Those who danced were thought to be quite insane by those who could not hear the music."

I've thought about that poster many times as I've sat in youth testimony meetings and heard a fine young man or a fine young woman (like you) talk about how their friends think they're strange because they get up long before sunrise and go to seminary. Or about their friends who don't understand why people like us would even consider going on a mission for no pay. Or they wonder why we won't drink, or party, or why we want to save our affections before marriage. I suppose they think we are quite insane, because they cannot "hear the music." Well, our job is to help them hear the beautiful music of the gospel. Many of them would like to "tune in" to this station on their spiritual radio, but they "know not where to find it" (see D&C 123:12).

What is that music? What is it that pulls us out of bed for early-morning seminary? (No, not your mother, that's not what I mean.) What is that feeling inside that makes us want to be better—not better looking, or more popular, but just

better? Back in the Orientation part of this book, I mentioned a fireside I attended, remember? There was such a
nice, calm feeling in the chapel that no one wanted to leave.
The fireside was over, and the dance was starting in the
gym, but no one seemed to want to go. I believe that many
of the youth in attendance were feeling the Spirit. I also
believe that many of them had felt it before, but this time,
they *recognized* it. They *knew* it felt different than the feeling of watching a movie or jumping around at a dance. It
was a quiet feeling, but it made you think. It made you think
about where you were going in your life, and it even told
you things that you should do. I could see it in their faces.
Inside, I know they were feeling things like, "I need to say
my prayers," or "I need to change my attitude," or "I want
to be clean." I believe that most of the youth stayed in the
chapel—when refreshments, socializing, and dancing were
only a few steps outside the door—because they wanted to
remember. They knew they were feeling something real, and
they wanted to remember what it felt like. I don't blame
them! Strong, impressive spiritual experiences really don't
come very often.

Sometimes, at firesides or in sacrament meetings or other
places, we get the wrong message. Speakers in Church
meetings often share their most powerful spiritual experiences, or the most powerful spiritual experiences of someone else. Those experiences are nice, and they inspire us.
But if we're not careful, we may think, "Wow. Nothing like
that has ever happened to me. I guess I've never felt the
Spirit."

That's the wrong message to get. We enjoy hearing about
other people's spiritual experiences, but we must be careful
to remember that really powerful spiritual experiences don't
happen very often. We shouldn't be discouraged! Listen to
this next quote: "I have learned that strong, impressive spiritual experiences do not come to us very frequently." Who

do you suppose said that? Me? My home teacher? Someone who doesn't feel the Spirit very often? No. It was an *apostle,* Elder Boyd K. Packer! This is an *apostle* saying that strong, impressive spiritual experiences do not come to us very frequently! Listen to what else he taught:

> The Spirit does not get our attention by shouting or shaking us with a heavy hand. Rather it whispers. It caresses so gently that if we are preoccupied we may not feel it at all. . . .
>
> Occasionally it will press just firmly enough for us to pay heed. But most of the time, if we do not heed the gentle feeling, the Spirit will withdraw and wait until we come seeking and listening.[1]

So the Spirit does not always speak with a loud and booming voice. More often, it is a *still small* voice. In fact, it's so still and small that "if we are preoccupied we may not feel it at all." Wow.

May I be bold for a minute? Do you think we could ever feel the Spirit in the middle of watching some empty and idiotic TV show? Or during an immoral or violent movie? What about a few hours later, when the images and feelings from those shows are still with us?

As you know, you feel more comfortable with some people than with others. Some people you can be with all day long, and they never make you feel uncomfortable. We have a word for such people: we call them "friends." I had missionary companions who were friends. Some of them were Filipino elders. We were different in so many ways! Our backgrounds, our eating and sleeping habits, the way we talked or expressed ourselves were all different. But I felt totally comfortable with them, and they with me. Why? Because Elder Perez and Elder Casinillo knew that I would never tell an off-color joke, or offer them a beer, or anything like that. We had the gospel in common, and that was all we needed.

Now, are you ready for a new thought? Here it comes. Do you think the Spirit of the Lord might be like that? Do you think that the Spirit of the Lord may simply feel more comfortable dwelling with some people than with others? Back when I was a junior in high school, I attended a camp with some other students. One of the camp counselors used the most profane and disgusting language I had ever heard in my life. I remember having to leave his presence several times because I literally became sick to my stomach. I didn't know that mere words could make me sick.

Similarly, if someone's thoughts are full of prime-time filth and immoral song lyrics, do you think the Spirit can feel *comfortable* with that person? To put it a little irreverently, I think it would make the Spirit sick, and cause him to leave.

Someone once said that the gospel is here to "comfort the afflicted, and afflict the comfortable." This next quote from Brigham Young has a tendency to "afflict the comfortable." Brace yourself (this is great):

> Pray the Lord to inspire your hearts. Ask for wisdom and knowledge. It is our duty to seek after it. Let us seek, and we shall find. . . . But as for His coming down here to pour His Spirit upon you, while you are aiming after the vain and frivolous things of the world [*Baywatch,* for example]; indulging in all the vanity, nonsense, and foolery which surrounds you [*Models Inc.*]; drinking in all the filthy abomination which should be spurned from every community on the earth [*Melrose Place*]—so long as you continue in this course, *rest assured He will not come near you.*[2]

As you may have guessed, Brigham Young didn't mention those TV shows in his quote. I inserted those. (If you don't recognize them, they've probably been cancelled—I hope.) And no, I've never seen those shows, only the commercials that highlight the featured immorality of the latest episode:

> *Tonight, in an all-star line-up, you'll never guess who winds up with who. . . . Yes, tonight, the truth and values you embrace will be mocked on every hand! Get hooked! Join us at 8:00 Central/7:00 Pacific.*

Okay, they don't really say that, but they might as well. But let's rewind for a second, and go back to the Brigham Young quote—did you hear that last part? *"Rest assured— [the Spirit] will not come near you!"* Why not? Because it would be too "uncomfortable." So what's the point of all this? The point is, we need to do the work necessary to be prepared to feel the Spirit of the Lord before we can feel it. We need to be doing our best to keep the commandments. We need to be in places where the Spirit can come. We need to be clean! To be filthy is to be weak:

> And they saw that they had become weak, like unto their brethren, the Lamanites, and that the Spirit of the Lord did no more preserve them; yea, it had withdrawn from them because *the Spirit of the Lord doth not dwell in unholy temples.* (Helaman 4:24; emphasis added)
>
> *And he doth not dwell in unholy temples;* neither can filthiness or anything which is unclean be received into the kingdom of God; therefore, I say unto you the time shall come, yea, and it shall be at the last day, that he who is filthy shall remain in his filthiness. (Alma 7:21; emphasis added)

HOW DOES THE SPIRIT SPEAK TO US?

As a junior in high school, I found myself one afternoon at the bowling alley with some friends. I rented a pair of lovely, high-fashion bowling shoes, chose a bowling ball, and waited for my turn. As I stood ready to deliver my ball down the lane, I noticed the little lighted number "11" at the end of the lane just above the pins. I was puzzled. Usually, you'll see a little number 1, indicating that this is your first ball. Well, to me, it looked like an 11. I squinted, and contorted my face, and the little green number 11 "morphed" into a number 1, and then back to a number 11. This was the first time I realized I needed glasses. I had always wanted to be a fighter pilot, but without 20-20 vision, I would have to settle for something else (but that's another story).

A few days later, I stood in the eye doctor's office and put on my new glasses for the first time. It was great. I looked out the window at billboard advertisements, and I was surprised at how sharp and clear they appeared. I could read the stenciled letters on the dumpster in the parking lot! And the next time I went bowling, I watched that 11 merge into a sharp and clear number 1. I repeatedly took off and put on my glasses and watched the number go from blurry to clear.

Why the bowling story? Well, I think one of the most common ways we feel the Spirit is that it makes things go from blurry to clear—just like putting on glasses. When the Spirit is with us we can "see" better than before. The word often used in the scriptures is *enlighten*.

> Verily, I say unto you, I will impart unto you of my Spirit, which shall *enlighten* your mind, which shall fill your soul with joy. (D&C 11:13; emphasis added)
>
> Behold, thou knowest that thou hast inquired of me and I did *enlighten* thy mind; and now I tell thee these things that thou mayest know that thou hast been *enlightened* by the Spirit of truth. (D&C 6:15; emphasis added)
>
> For by my Spirit will I *enlighten* them, and by my power will I make known unto them the secrets of

> my will—yea, even those things which eye has not
> seen, nor ear heard, nor yet entered into the heart of
> man. (D&C 76:10; emphasis added)
>
> For my Spirit is sent forth into the world to *enlighten*
> the humble and contrite, and to the condemnation of
> the ungodly. (D&C 136:33; emphasis added)

I've often sat in meetings where I felt "enlightened." There
was no burning feeling, and no glorious vision, but the Spirit
was present nonetheless. Inside, I felt enlightened,
instructed. Everything became clear. "John," my thoughts
would say, "you need to do better on your scripture reading." Or, "John, you need to do better in your prayers."
Nephi's younger brother Jacob taught, "The Spirit speaketh
the truth and lieth not. Wherefore, it speaketh of things as
they really are, and of things as they really will be; wherefore, these things are manifested unto us plainly, for the salvation of our souls" (Jacob 4:13). That's the way it is. The
Spirit makes things plain.

I have also noticed that when I feel "enlightened," I sometimes feel a little bit scolded. The Spirit seems to be saying,
"John, you can do better, and you know it." I guess I don't
mind being scolded in these situations. Elder Neal A.
Maxwell said, "When conscience calls to us from the next
ridge, it is not solely to scold but also to beckon."[3] That
"scolding" is the Spirit beckoning me to do better. "C'mon,
John. Come up to higher ground. You can do better. You
can *be* better!" I absolutely love it when I have this feeling. I
know I make my best decisions under its influence, and I
want to feel it as often as I can. That's why this is one of my
favorite quotes:

> Men are mortal and beset by human frailties. . . .
> When they are under the influence of an exalted
> occasion, they make high resolves. They firmly
> determine to avoid past mistakes and to do better.

But gone out from under the spell of that influence and absorbed in the complicated pursuits of life, they find difficulty in holding fast to their noble purposes. . . . *So it is essential that they come again, and frequently, under the influence which kindles anew the warmth of spirit in which good resolutions are begotten*, that they may go out fortified to withstand the pressures of temptation which lure them into false ways. Happily, *if they refresh themselves frequently enough* under ennobling influences, the spirit of repentance will be at work with them, and they will make conquest of some temptations—rise above them—and advance thus far toward their final goal.[4]

That was a long quote, but did you catch the main message? *"Come again, and frequently!"* To me, this quote says that if we want to feel those "enlightening" moments, we need to take advantage of every chance we have to feel the Spirit—every opportunity to attend a fireside, a standards night, our Sunday meetings, and our family home evenings; every opportunity we have to attend seminary, read our scriptures, listen to good music, watch Church videos. Every opportunity we have to make our thoughts go from blurry to clear, we need to take it!

When it comes to matters of the Spirit, we need to be careful not to compare ourselves to others too much. Some people seem to think that the Spirit affects everyone the same way. For example, some may believe that "whoever cries the most is the most spiritual," and that's not necessarily true. For some people, the presence of the Spirit may bring tears. For others it doesn't. You may feel the Spirit very strongly and not shed any tears at all. Some may confuse strong emotion for the Spirit. Elder Boyd K. Packer said:

The spiritual part of us and the emotional part of us are so closely linked that it is possible to mistake an emotional impulse for something spiritual. We occasionally find people who receive what they assume to be spiritual promptings from God, when those promptings are either centered in the emotions or are from the adversary.[5]

If I had one thing to say to teenagers about recognizing the Spirit, it would be this: "Be patient, be clean, and don't give up." This is a difficult topic to write about, because I feel like I'm just *beginning* to understand how the Spirit works in my life—and I'm already ___ years old! (I'm not going to tell you how old I am, but if you're a teenager, I'm older than you.)

In the April 1989 *Ensign*, there is an excellent article titled "Have I Received an Answer from the Spirit?" In this article, Brother Jay E. Jensen outlines several different ways the Spirit may communicate with us. The Spirit:

1. Speaks peace to the mind
2. Causes the bosom to burn
3. Tells us in our minds and our hearts
4. Comes as a voice in the mind
5. Leads us to do something
6. Occupies our minds and presses upon our feelings
7. Constrains us from dangerous or improper things

As we go through this list, I bet you'll remember times when the Spirit has helped you. Let's talk about each one for a minute.

1. The Spirit speaks peace to the mind. The Spirit can bring peace, calmness, and tranquillity. It can remove turmoil and anxious feelings. The Lord answered one of Oliver Cowdery's prayers by sending a feeling of peace. This is interesting: Later, the Lord gave Oliver a revelation to inform him that he had already received a revelation!

> Verily, verily, I say unto you, if you desire a further witness, cast your mind upon the night that you cried unto me in your heart, that you might know concerning the truth of these things.
>
> Did I not speak peace to your mind concerning the matter? What greater witness can you have than from God?
>
> And now, behold, you have received a witness; for if I have told you things which no man knoweth have you not received a witness? (D&C 6:22–23)

Jesus is the "Prince of Peace" (Isaiah 9:6), and he spoke to his disciples about peace:

> Peace I leave with you, my peace I give unto you: not as the world giveth, give I unto you. Let not your heart be troubled, neither let it be afraid. (John 14:27)

2. The Spirit causes the bosom to burn. After Jesus was resurrected, he walked with two of his disciples on the road to Emmaus. He talked with them for a while, and then left. They didn't recognize him when he was with them, but after he left they said, "Did not our heart burn within us, while he talked with us by the way, and while he opened to us the scriptures?" (Luke 24:32).

Don't be too discouraged if you've never felt this warm feeling. Because of the wonderful counsel given to Oliver Cowdery in Doctrine and Covenants section 9, many have felt like spiritual misfits if they have never experienced the "burning in the bosom." In the article mentioned above, Brother Jensen relates the following story, shared by a member of the Quorum of the Seventy:

> One of the Quorum of the Twelve came to tour the mission over which the Seventy was presiding. As they drove to the next zone conference, the Apostle turned to him and said, "I wonder if you might have

left an impression in the missionaries' minds that has created more problems than you can resolve. As I have traveled throughout the Church, I've found relatively few people who have experienced a burning of the bosom. In fact, I've had many people tell me that they've become frustrated because they have never experienced that feeling even though they have prayed or fasted for long periods of time."

He explained that Doctrine and Covenants 9:7–9 was given in response to the process of translating sacred records. There the burning of the bosom was appropriate. The principle can apply to personal revelation, he said, but more precisely it related to the translation of the Book of Mormon. He counseled the mission president to refer missionaries to other scriptural references about the Holy Ghost. For example, he cited the verse "Did not I speak peace to your mind concerning the matter? What greater witness can you have than from God?"[6]

3. The Spirit tells us in our minds and hearts. I spent a lot of time on this one earlier in the chapter, because I believe it is the most common way we feel the Spirit. When the Spirit speaks to our minds and hearts, we are "enlightened" and things become clear. The Lord told Oliver Cowdery, "Yea, behold, I will tell you in your mind and in your heart, by the Holy Ghost, which shall come upon you and which shall dwell in your heart" (D&C 8:2). Not only do things make sense in our minds, but they feel right in our hearts. I think that's why the scripture says mind *and* heart.

4. The Spirit comes as a voice in the mind. President David O. McKay has said that the Holy Ghost speaks through the conscience of the members of the Church who are in the line of their duty. Most people's thoughts are in their own voice, and when thoughts come into your mind, it may be hard to distinguish between your own voice and the Spirit of the Lord. Others times it may be very clear that the "voice" came from somewhere else. Brother Jensen continues:

> At times, a person may actually hear an audible voice; at other times, a person may have an impression or a thought come into his mind expressed in one or more complete sentences. Enos reported that while he was "struggling in the spirit, behold, the voice of the Lord came into [his] mind." (Enos 1:10.)[7]

5. The Spirit leads us to do something. This is another common way that the Spirit influences us. I'm sure you've heard stories about someone who "felt impressed" to make a phone call, or visit someone, or do a favor for someone, and it turned out that the person really needed that service at that time. You may have even been led by the Spirit to say "hi" to someone at school, or to keep someone company who was having a hard day. The Spirit can lead you to do these things.

I remember attending a very rowdy Scout meeting one Tuesday night many years ago. Our Scoutmaster was doing his best to teach us about the Citizenship in the World merit badge, but we were bouncing off the walls. He did what he could to explain the requirements, but we were being totally obnoxious. He finally finished and asked someone to give the prayer. With my head bowed, I remember feeling like something was wrong. I watched my Scoutmaster putting away his things after the prayer, and I felt bad. Something— I believe it was the Spirit—told me that he felt like he had failed. I determined that I would go home and work on that merit badge until I earned it. I wanted my Scoutmaster to know that I did not ignore all his work that night.

The Lord told Hyrum Smith:

> And now, verily, verily, I say unto thee, put your trust in that Spirit which leadeth to do good—yea, to

do justly, to walk humbly, to judge righteously; and
this is my Spirit. (D&C 11:12)

That may seem like a simple scripture, but it's important
to emphasize that the Spirit leads us to do *good*. If someone
says something like, "The Spirit led me to slug my little
brother," or "The Spirit told me not to listen to the prophet,"
I think you can know it's not the Spirit of the Lord. The
prophet Mormon gave us a key for how to judge if a
prompting comes from the Spirit of the Lord or the spirit of
the devil:

> But behold, that which is of God inviteth and
> enticeth to do good continually; wherefore, every
> thing which inviteth and enticeth to do good, and to
> love God, and to serve him, is inspired of God. . . .
> But whatsoever thing persuadeth men to do evil,
> and believe not in Christ, and deny him, and serve
> not God, then ye may know with a perfect knowl-
> edge it is of the devil; for after this manner doth the
> devil work, for he persuadeth no man to do good,
> no, not one; neither do his angels; neither do they
> who subject themselves unto him. (Moroni 7:13, 17)

Some people are deceived and even leave the Church
because they are confused in this area. They may think they
have been given a "higher law." They may suddenly feel that
they are more entitled to inspiration than the leaders of the
Church. The Spirit would not tell anyone to go against the
prophet and leave the Church. Sorry, folks, it's just not going
to happen. If they knew the scriptures, they would know
they had been deceived. Remember, as the Primary song
says, "Follow the prophet"! President Wilford Woodruff said:

> The Lord will never permit me or any other man
> who stands as President of this Church to lead you
> astray. It is not in the programme. It is not in the

mind of God. If I were to attempt that, the Lord would remove me out of my place, and so He will any other man who attempts to lead the children of men astray from the oracles of God and from their duty.[8]

One of the reasons I love to watch general conference is because I know that if I listen to the prophet, and follow him, I will not be led astray.

6. *The Spirit occupies our minds and presses upon our feelings.* I love to read Joseph Smith's testimony. You'll remember that he read from the book of James, "If any of you lack wisdom, let him ask of God" (James 1:5). Once he'd read that verse, he couldn't get it out of his mind! Listen to his own words:

> Never did any passage of scripture come with more power to the heart of man than this did at this time to mine. It seemed to enter with great force into every feeling of my heart. I reflected on it again and again, knowing that if any person needed wisdom from God, I did. (Joseph Smith–History 1:12)

The Spirit of the Lord was telling Joseph that this verse was important. Many sections of the Doctrine and Covenants were revealed after the Prophet was impressed to meditate and ponder about a certain subject for a long time.

In the same way, if *you* seem to be reflecting on something again and again, maybe the Lord is trying to tell you something too.

7. *The Spirit constrains us from dangerous or improper things.* Many years ago, my brother David was driving to a party up Emigration Canyon. Suddenly, a feeling came over him that he should turn around and go home. So he turned around and headed back. But then he started to think, "They're expecting me, they're waiting for me, and they'll be worried if I don't show up," so he turned around and started

back up the canyon. The feeling came again, "Turn around and go home." So he turned around and headed home again. But the same objections arose in his mind. This time David stopped the car, knelt down, and prayed. He told the Lord that he felt he was getting promptings from the Spirit, but that people were waiting for him, and he needed to go. He told the Lord, however, that if he felt the prompting again, he would head home with no more questions. The Lord seemed to let him continue this time, but David knew something was wrong at that party, because the Lord had warned him. When David arrived, he found that there *was* something wrong, and that he needed to get out of there. He stayed long enough to persuade two of his friends to get in the car, and the three of them drove home.

When I was on my mission, many times I would get a feeling that I shouldn't go to certain places. Sometimes I would think, "Was that my own thoughts or the Spirit?" When the feeling seemed to come out of nowhere, I obeyed. I don't know what would have happened if I had ignored the Spirit on those occasions, but that's not the point. The point is, follow the Spirit when it constrains! It's smarter than you are!

A FEW CLOSING THOUGHTS

As I have tried to learn how to recognize and use the Spirit in my life, I have been motivated by the words of Nephi. I have heard people say, "I don't think I've ever felt the Spirit, and I'm not going to do anything until I do!" or "I'll wait until the Lord tells me *exactly* what to do." Nephi, on the other hand, had a different approach. He was willing to *move*, full of faith that the Lord would guide him when he needed it. In 1 Nephi 4:6 we read, "And I was led by the Spirit, *not knowing beforehand* the things which I should do" (emphasis added). Nephi was a man of action. Nephi said, "I will go and do," not "I will sit and stew." Elder Marion G. Romney agreed with this approach: "While the

Lord will magnify us in both subtle and dramatic ways, he can only guide our footsteps when we move our feet."[9] If you want to feel the Spirit, you've got to move your feet!

Remember to be patient. Sometimes it seems as if the Lord waits until the last possible second before sending his inspiration. "And it shall be given thee in the very moment what thou shalt speak and write" (D&C 24:6). There have been times in my life when I have begged and pleaded for guidance and felt as if I received nothing. Months later I have looked back and realized that I was being guided all along—that my prayers *had* been heard by the Lord. I realized that "as often as [I] inquired . . . [I] received instruction of [the] Spirit" (D&C 6:14). So be patient, purify your life, and keep the faith. The Lord will speak to you in his own way and in his own time.

There's one more important thing about the Spirit that I'd like to mention before we're done. Some people think the Spirit is just a "good feeling." And it is, but it's more than that. If the Spirit were only a good feeling, it would be nothing more than "background music" to life. But the Spirit is much more than background music. I believe the Spirit is more like the phone ringing. It needs to be answered! My seminary-teacher friend Bill Carpenter is fond of saying, "The Spirit of the Lord is a call to action, and the action you take is your answer to God." I agree. Whenever I've felt the Spirit, I've always felt as if I should *do* something! I've felt that I should take action in some way. I've felt that I want to repent, be clean, and change my heart and motives. And the action I take is my answer to God. So when you hear the phone ringing, answer it!

Learning to recognize and understand the Spirit is perhaps one of the most important goals you will ever have in your life. As President Ezra Taft Benson has stated, "The Lord can make a lot more out of your life than you can." You will need to know how to follow the Spirit to receive that help.

When you live your life by high standards, and desire with all your heart to be valiant, you will eventually gain respect from the people you admire most. Others may think you are insane, but that's only because they can't hear the music. Stay tuned—or, in other words, stay "in tune"—and you will be able to hear the soothing and motivating music of the Spirit. It will guide you through all of life's hazards, and take you all the way home to your Father in Heaven.

EXTRA CREDIT

"Have I Received an Answer from the Spirit?" Jay E. Jensen, *Ensign*, April 1989, pp. 21–25.

"Revelation," Dallin H. Oaks, *New Era*, September 1982, pp. 38–46.

"I Have a Question," Dallin H. Oaks, *Ensign*, June 1983, p. 27.

"Learning to Recognize Answers to Prayer," Richard G. Scott, *Ensign*, November 1989, pp. 30–32.

"Prayers and Answers," Boyd K. Packer, in *That All May be Edified* (Salt Lake City: Bookcraft, 1982), pp. 9–15.

"The Candle of the Lord," Boyd K. Packer, *Ensign*, January 1983, pp. 51–56.

"Understanding Personal Revelation," talk on cassette, Joseph Fielding McConkie (Salt Lake City: Deseret Book, 1991).

"Receiving Answers to Our Prayers," talk on cassette, Gene R. Cook (Salt Lake City: Deseret Book, 1991).

FOURTH PERIOD ENDNOTES

Division page quotation: Neal A. Maxwell, *Ensign*, November 1976, p. 14.

1. Boyd K. Packer, *Ensign*, January 1983, p. 53.
2. Brigham Young, *Journal of Discourses*, 1:120; emphasis in original.
3. Neal A. Maxwell, *Ensign*, November 1976, p. 14.
4. Albert E. Bowen, cited by Dean L. Larsen, *Ensign*, November 1989, p. 62.
5. Boyd K. Packer, *Ensign*, January 1983, p. 56.

6. Jay E. Jensen, *Ensign,* April 1989, pp. 21–22.
7. Ibid., p. 23.
8. Wilford Woodruff, Doctrine and Covenants, Official Declaration 1.
9. Marion G. Romney, *Ensign,* May 1981, p. 91.

Communications 101

Improving Your Prayers

Prayer can solve more problems, alleviate more suffering, prevent more transgression, and bring about greater peace and contentment in the human soul than can be obtained in any other way.
—Thomas S. Monson

Let's play a guessing game, okay? I'm thinking of something—an event. Your job is to guess what it is. Are you ready? I'll give you a few clues:

Because of this event, you are reading this book.

Because of this event, hundreds of thousands of the world's best teenagers get up before the sun rises and go to seminary before school starts.

Because of this event, thousands of men, women, and children endured unbelievable hardship and walked across a continent.

Today, even as we speak, fifty thousand young men and women have left their homes to teach people all over the world about this event for no pay.

Because of this event, millions are familiar with the names "Nephi," "Alma," and "Moroni."

Because of this event, the whole world has been changed. The priesthood of God has been restored, baptism by immersion for the remission of sins is available, and families can be sealed together forever.

Because of this event, millions of people will endure whatever persecutions or hardships come their way as they watch and wait for the second coming of Jesus Christ to the earth.

What is this remarkable, amazing, powerful event that has changed the whole world forever?

The prayer of a teenager.

That's it. The prayer of a fourteen-year-old farm boy back in 1820 changed the world, and it will never be the same. The point? *Don't ever underestimate the power of prayer.* The

Father and the Son appeared to Joseph Smith in the spring of 1820 because of his faithful response to a beautiful scripture: "If any of you lack wisdom, let him ask of God, that giveth to all men liberally, and upbraideth not; and it shall be given him" (James 1:5).

Sometimes it seems like the answer to every question in Sunday School is "pray and read your scriptures." Well, that's good advice, because that's exactly what young Joseph Smith did, and because he did, the world is a different place today.

DON'T EVER STOP PRAYING

Prayer is so important that if you're not praying twice a day, the President of the Church may be fearful for you! Are you on his worry list? This is what President Heber J. Grant said:

> I have little or no fear for the . . . young man or the young woman, who honestly and conscientiously supplicate God twice a day for the guidance of His Spirit.[1]

I believe there's more to that quote than meets the eye. Is President Grant saying that all you have to do is pray twice a day and everything will be fine? No—he said he has little fear for you if you are *already* praying twice a day. What's the difference? I'll tell you. Usually, when people are having a tough time, struggling with sin, or bordering on inactivity, what's one of the first things they stop doing? Right! They stop praying. I've met many young people who are still attending seminary and church, but who have stopped praying. Everything may appear fine on the outside, but inside they are struggling. I think that President Grant is saying that if you are praying twice a day, he has little fear for you because the other things in your life are probably all right.

Why do people stop praying? I don't know—there are probably as many reasons as there are people. But I would like to make a guess at one of those reasons. I met a young woman once who said she hadn't really prayed in months.

She said the blessing on the food when she was asked to, and she said opening prayers in seminary and Sunday School classes, but she offered no personal prayers. When I asked her why, she looked at the ground and explained, "Well, I've made a lot of mistakes in my life, and I've done some things, and I don't see why Heavenly Father would listen to me, 'cause I've done so many dumb things."

"Yes indeed, friends, Heavenly Father will only listen to perfect people, so I guess it's no use." If that were the case, who could pray? I couldn't. Nobody could! We make the dumb but common mistake of assigning God some truly imperfect traits if we think he listens only to perfect people. What kind of a father would that be? It's *Satan* who wants you to believe that way. He wants you to think that you can't pray unless you're perfect. Let's listen again to one of the people I respect most—Nephi:

> For if ye would hearken unto the Spirit which teacheth a man to pray ye would know that ye must pray; for the evil spirit teacheth not a man to pray, but teacheth him that he must not pray.
> But behold, I say unto you that ye must pray always, and not faint. (2 Nephi 32:8–9)

In other words, if you ever have that feeling that you can't pray, now you know where it comes from. It isn't from God. He always wants you to pray. It comes from "the evil spirit."

Of course, it's easier to say that than to believe it. When we've made a big mistake, or when we've sinned, it's much harder to pray. I know that. But that's also the most important time to keep in touch with our Heavenly Father. He knows what we've done. We're not going to surprise him.

If you find that it's really hard to pray, don't tell your friends, tell your Father! You might say, "Heavenly Father, this is really hard for me to do. I know I'm not perfect, and I've made some mistakes, but thou hast a commandment to pray, so here I am." That kind of prayer is remarkably similar to a prayer spoken by the brother of Jared. Listen to how humble he is:

> Now behold, O Lord, and do not be angry with thy servant because of his weakness before thee; for we know that thou art holy and dwellest in the heavens, and that we are unworthy before thee; because of the fall our natures have become evil continually; nevertheless, O Lord, thou hast given us a commandment that we must call upon thee, that from thee we may receive according to our desires. (Ether 3:2)

What if the brother of Jared had thought, "Oh, well, I'm not worthy, so I won't pray." Or, "I'll just forget about praying until I'm perfect." As a matter of fact, it so happens that the brother of Jared *did* forget to pray for a while, and what do you think happened? He got scolded for *three hours!*

> And it came to pass at the end of four years that the Lord came again unto the brother of Jared, and stood in a cloud and talked with him. And for the space of three hours did the Lord talk with the brother of Jared, and chastened him because he remembered not to call upon the name of the Lord. (Ether 2:14)

Perhaps you're thinking, "Well, I'm not as important as the brother of Jared. I still wonder if God hears my prayers." You know, I'm glad you said that, because I've just been waiting to give you another quote. Presiding Bishop H. Burke Peterson said this:

> I want you to know that I know that whenever one of Heavenly Father's children kneels and talks to him, he listens. I know this as well as I know anything in this world—that Heavenly Father listens to every prayer from his children. I know our prayers ascend

to heaven. *No matter what we may have done wrong, he listens to us.*[2]

So let's just dispense with the ridiculous little "I-don't-think-God-listens-to-me" comments. I've had it with that stuff! It's not true now, and it never was true. The important thing is that you pray. You don't have to be perfect to be heard, and you don't have to pray perfectly. For now, the most important thing is that you try, okay? Now, let's get down to business.

WE KNOW WE CAN DO BETTER IN OUR PERSONAL PRAYERS

A young woman once told me, "I pray, but I don't feel anything." At first I wanted to say, "Well, welcome to the club." As we learned in Fourth Period, strong and impressive spiritual experiences do not come to us very often. Perhaps you're different from me, but I would say I only feel things in my prayers maybe 2 or 3 percent of the time. Not very often. But I *know* God is there, and I will *never* stop praying.

This chapter is not intended to teach anyone how to pray. I imagine whoever is out there reading this book already knows the basic steps to prayer. This chapter is intended to motivate us to try harder, and to make our personal prayers a more important part of our day. The problem is, sometimes you and I (guilty sigh) are simply not doing our best in our personal prayers. We've fallen into a routine. What we need is a gentle (or maybe a not-so-gentle) reminder of what we already know. Sometimes we're simply not concentrating on improving the quality of our prayers.

Let's imagine it. You get home late, you kneel down by the side of your bed—wait a minute, you are kneeling, aren't you? You're not just lying on your back and looking toward heaven and expecting to stay awake? If you're praying like that, you'll fall asleep in the middle of your prayers. Then you'll wake up and look at your clock at 2:00 A.M. and say, "Um . . . um . . . Amen! Wow, that was a long one." I don't think that counts for much.

Okay, so you *kneel* down by your bed. A note of caution here: when you kneel down, don't just do a "face plant" into the mattress. I've done that before when I've started to pray, but sometimes, when I'm really tired, my thoughts begin to drift. At first I'm praying, but after a while I become lost in La-La Land. And I hate to tell you this, but I've thought and said some of the weirdest things in the middle of my prayers. How embarrassing! Has that ever happened to you? When you finally realize where you are, that you're on your knees next to your bed, it hits you that you were in the middle of praying! Isn't it embarrassing at that point when you have to say, "Oh . . . sorry, Heavenly Father—um—bless the sick and the afflicted . . . " This may be a little irreverent, but I wonder if Father isn't thinking, "I'd like to afflict you! Then maybe you'd remember me, and pray with a little more intent!"

> And thus we see that except the Lord doth chasten his people with many afflictions, yea, except he doth visit them with death and with terror, and with famine and with all manner of pestilence, they will not remember him. (Helaman 12:3)

You've probably heard the saying, "There are no atheists in foxholes." Yup. When the crisis is on, watch people get religious. We must be sure that we are praying not only in the tough times, but when things are easy and life is good. Elder Howard W. Hunter said:

> If prayer is only a spasmodic cry at the time of crisis, then it is utterly selfish, and we come to think of God as a repairman or a service agency to help us only in our emergencies.[3]

Imagine if you were looking down on this world, and

knew that only a small fraction of your children would kneel and talk to you at the end of the day. That's a sad thought, isn't it? Let's you and I commit to pray morning and night, in good times and bad, okay?

OPEN THE DOOR!

At one time or another, you've probably seen a painting of Jesus knocking on a door. I can recall three different versions of that painting. We had one in our house when I was growing up. I remember my dad asking me when I was very young, "John, what is different about this door?" I looked at it as closely as I could, but couldn't find anything unusual. "Keep looking," my dad said. Finally, I noticed that there was no doorknob! I said, "Oh, there's no handle!" And my dad said, "That's right. Do you know why?" I didn't, but I studied it some more, and finally my dad said, "If you want Jesus to come in, *you* have to open the door." The scripture that inspired that painting comes from Revelation 3:20: "Behold, I stand at the door, and knock: if any man hear my voice, and open the door, I will come in to him."

In other scriptures, the situation is reversed: We are at the door, and we do the knocking. For example: "Draw near unto me and I will draw near unto you; seek me diligently and ye shall find me; ask, and ye shall receive; knock, and it shall be opened unto you" (D&C 88:63). There are some wonderful principles in there. Let's examine this scripture in a more visual way:

WHERE YOU ARE:	WHERE GOD IS:
Draw near unto me ■	■ and I will draw near unto you;
seek me diligently ■	■ and ye shall find me;
ask, ■	■ and ye shall receive;
knock, ■	■ and it shall be opened unto you.

Now, what have you noticed? With every action you take, you move closer to the Lord, and he can move closer to you!

But there's something more important. In every case, guess who has to move first? *You do!* Someone once said, "If you feel farther away from God today than you were yesterday, you can be sure who moved." It's true. If you want to be closer to the Lord, you have to *move* closer! You may be asking, "How do you seek, ask, and knock?" Good question. Now we'll give some examples and become even more visual:

WHAT YOU DO:	WHAT GOD DOES:
Draw near unto me ■ *(be obedient)*	■ and I will draw near unto you;
seek me diligently ■ *(study the scriptures)*	■ and ye shall find me;
ask, ■ *(pray faithfully)*	■ and ye shall receive;
knock, ■	■ and it shall be opened unto you.

See how that works? Now, I know that you are a very polite person, and you would not barge in on a party where you were not invited. In the same way, Heavenly Father respects our free agency enough that he will not go where he's not invited. He will wait for us to move closer to him through obedience and prayer. And when we do, he has promised he will move closer to us.

The opposite is also true. You've seen how obedience can bring us closer to the Lord. What do you suppose disobedience would do? Let's take a look.

IF YOU AND I:	WHERE GOD IS:
"veg" on irrelevant, immoral TV, ■	■
disrespect members of our family, ■	■
and adopt a "how-bad-can-I-be" attitude, ■	■

then we "draw away" from God! And we distance ourselves

from the influence of his Spirit. Remember? "The Spirit of the Lord doth not dwell in unholy temples" (Helaman 4:24). With every activity, every day, we either draw closer to God or move farther away from him.

BE PERSISTENT AND CONSISTENT

One day I was waiting in line at the grocery store. I was behind a mom and a little boy. Moms are known for being able to do about 47 million things at once, and this mom was no different. She was conversing with the cashier, filling out a check with her right hand, and with her left hand holding by the wrist a hyper little boy who was struggling to get away. He was just out of reach of a display of candy bars. When he realized that he couldn't reach them by himself, he stopped trying to pull away, stepped close to his mother's side, and started tugging on her coat. "Mom?" (tug, tug, tug, tug). *"Mom?"* (tug, tug, tug). "MOM!" (tug, tug). At this point, the little boy put all his weight on his left foot, fixed his gaze on the ceiling, and put it on automatic: "Mom (tug) Mom (tug) Mom (tug) Mom (tug) Mom (tug) Mom (tug) Mom (tug) Mom (tug) . . . " Finally the mother, obviously ruffled, turned and answered, *"What?"* At this point the boy pointed to his left and said something like, "Nestle's Crunch!" I almost broke out laughing. Then I thought, "How perfect! I could use this in a talk!" (That's why I'm telling you about it now.) I'm hoping that you listened to that story with your spiritual ears, and you know what I'm going to say.

The boy wanted something, and he knew he couldn't get it by himself. He looked to a higher power, but got no response after a few tries. Very determined, he fixed his eyes upward and tugged and tugged until he got an answer. As I witnessed this event, I was reminded of something Joseph Smith said: "Weary [the Lord] until he blesses you."[4] Isn't that interesting? "Weary the Lord." In other words, be persistent. Let him know you're there! Sometimes, in our prayers, we say, "Father?" (tug, tug, tug, tug). *"Father?"* (tug, tug, tug).

"FATHER!" (tug, tug). Then we say to ourselves as we hit the pillow to go to sleep, "He just doesn't answer my prayers." Hmmm. I think we need to be more like that little boy and "weary the Lord." The boy knew that if he tugged long enough and hard enough, he would get his mother's attention. In the same way, if we tug long and hard, I believe the Lord will, in his own way and time, send us an answer. (See Luke 18:1–8.)

Perhaps the Lord will let us pray for a certain blessing for weeks, months, or even years. But this kind of struggling will build our faith and our spiritual muscles, and make us more humble and aware of our dependence on him. At these times we need to trust him, and believe in him, and "be still and know that [he is] God" (D&C 101:16).

AVOID VAIN REPETITION

You've probably heard the story of the man who was asked to offer a prayer at a prison. Because he was in the habit of using some of the same words and phrases in his prayers, he said, "We're thankful for this beautiful building we have to meet in, and we hope that those who are not here will be here next time . . . " Oops. Brother Jack Marshall talks about how we might prepare an ice-cream sundae, full of fat and refined sugar, and drenched with chocolate syrup. Then we bow our heads and ask the Lord to bless it to "nourish and strengthen our bodies." Oops again.

"Vain repetition" means using the same phrases over and over in our prayers without really meaning or thinking about what we are saying. Of course, it is fine to thank the Lord for a beautiful building to meet in, and to ask him to bless our food that it will nourish and strengthen us, if that's what we really mean. The key is sincerity. When prayers become just a habit, and we don't invest any real concentration and effort, then we are guilty of vain repetition. President Ezra Taft Benson said:

> Our prayers should be meaningful and pertinent.
> . . . Do not use the same phrases at each prayer. Each
> of us would become disturbed if a friend said the
> same words to us each day, treated the conversation
> as a chore, and could hardly wait to finish in order to
> turn on the TV and forget us.[5]

I remember that, as a boy, I felt I should go down the list
of everyone in the family and ask the Lord to bless them.
After a while, I thought of a more "efficient" prayer. I
remember telling my older brother how quickly I could bless
a large number of people. I would say, "Please bless everyone I know, and everyone I've ever seen." Fortunately, I
grew up, and I no longer treat the Lord like a servant who
needs a "to-do" list from me.

Sometimes, when things are tough in my life, I don't even
know what to say in my prayers. And do you know what?
That's okay. Sometimes we don't even need words to pray.

> Likewise the Spirit also helpeth our infirmities: for
> we know not what we should pray for as we ought:
> but the Spirit itself maketh intercession for us with
> groanings which cannot be uttered. (Romans 8:26)

Even if we can't find the words, the Lord knows what we
need. And this kind of prayer, though it may be more feelings than words, will reach heaven much easier than one full
of vain repetition. Once again, the test is our sincerity, our
intent. Mormon warned:

> And likewise also is it counted evil unto a man, if
> he shall pray and not with real intent of heart; yea,
> and it profiteth him nothing, for God receiveth none
> such. (Moroni 7:9)

WHO LISTENS TO, AND WHO ANSWERS OUR PRAYERS?

A young woman wrote and asked me, "Do Heavenly
Father and Jesus listen when we pray, or just Heavenly

Father?" Good question. We know that Jesus prayed very often while he was on the earth, and he told the Nephites, "Therefore ye must always pray unto the Father in my name" (3 Nephi 18:19). We know that we address our prayers to our Father in Heaven. As to whether Jesus hears them too, let's read what Elder Bruce R. McConkie wrote:

> It is true that when we pray to the Father, the answer comes from the Son, because "there is . . . one mediator between God and men, the man Christ Jesus." (1 Timothy 2:5.) Joseph Smith, for instance, asked the Father, in the name of the Son, for answers to questions, and the answering voice was not that of the Father but of the Son, because Christ is our advocate, our intercessor, the God (under the Father) who rules and regulates this earth. . . .
>
> But what we must have perfectly clear is that we *always* pray to the Father, not the Son, and we *always* pray in the name of the Son.[6]

We don't know exactly how, but in some way our prayers are conveyed to the Son so that he may answer us. He also sends the Holy Ghost, or the Comforter, to answer our prayers. Jesus said, "But the Comforter, which is the Holy Ghost, whom the Father will send in my name, he shall teach you all things, and bring all things to your remembrance, whatsoever I have said unto you" (John 14:26).

WHAT SHOULD WE PRAY FOR?

As a little boy, I remember praying very hard one night for a bicycle. I bowed my head and prayed very earnestly for a bike to be sitting in my room when I looked up. I'd pray, and look up, then I'd pray some more, and look up. I prayed for quite a while, as I remember, while my brother slept in the bunk below. (I don't know how I would have explained it to him if a bike had appeared.)

I have since learned that we must be careful what we pray

for, and that we should always add "Thy will be done" in our prayers. Sometimes we pray for things that wouldn't be good for us, and fortunately, in those cases, we often don't get what we want. (You may have heard a country music song called "Thank Heaven for Unanswered Prayers.")

At a youth conference testimony meeting, a young woman told how she prayed every night to have a boyfriend. She was only fifteen, and not even old enough to begin dating, but she prayed and prayed and prayed to have a boyfriend. She thought this would make her happy. She said that the Lord finally answered her prayers by telling her that she "wouldn't be able to handle the things that would come with having a boyfriend." This was her personal answer to the question, "Why can't I date before I'm sixteen?" I was impressed with her honesty and sincerity. She learned that the Lord knew better than she did what would be right for her.

This brings up another important point: We are not promised that we will receive *everything* we pray for, but we are promised every *right* thing we pray for.

> Whatsoever ye shall ask the Father in my name, *which is right*, believing that ye shall receive, behold it shall be given unto you. (3 Nephi 18:20; emphasis added)
>
> Whatsoever ye ask the Father in my name it shall be given unto you, that is expedient for you. (D&C 88:64)

Do you know what *expedient* means? Hang on, I'll get the dictionary. . . . It says, "useful for effecting a desired result." Because Heavenly Father knows us better than we know ourselves, he also knows what's best for us, and what our "desired results" ought to be. Though at times it may seem he is not answering our prayers, it may be that he wants us to wait for something even better. Jesus taught:

What man is there of you, who, if his son ask bread, will give him a stone?

Or if he ask a fish, will he give him a serpent?

If ye then, being evil, know how to give good gifts unto your children, how much more shall your Father who is in heaven give good things to them that ask him? (3 Nephi 14:9–11)

What a beautiful thought. Our Father in heaven is willing to give good gifts to them that ask him. So what should we ask for? Do you want a list? Okay, fine, I'll give you one. Actually, it's Amulek's list from Alma 34, and it's great.

Yea, cry unto him for mercy; for he is mighty to save.

Yea, humble yourselves, and continue in prayer unto him.

Cry unto him when ye are in your fields, yea, over all your flocks.

Cry unto him in your houses, yea, over all your household, both morning, mid-day, and evening.

Yea, cry unto him against the power of your enemies.

Yea, cry unto him against the devil, who is an enemy to all righteousness.

Cry unto him over the crops of your fields, that ye may prosper in them.

Cry over the flocks of your fields, that they may increase.

But this is not all; ye must pour out your souls in your closets, and your secret places, and in your wilderness.

Yea, and when you do not cry unto the Lord, let your hearts be full, drawn out in prayer unto him continually for your welfare, and also for the welfare of those who are around you. (Alma 34:18–27)

By now you may be saying, "John, I don't have any fields, and I don't have any flocks, and I don't have any crops." Well, neither do I. So, let's do as Nephi recommended, and "liken all scriptures unto [ourselves]" (1 Nephi 19:23). What *do* you have? You may not be able to pray in your field over your flocks, but can you pray in school over your books? You may not work with crops in your field, but you may have peer pressure where you *do* work. You may not have your own household, but imagine the power you can have in your own family if, when you offer the family prayer, you mention your parents and each of your brothers and sisters by name, and lovingly pray for them. And if there isn't regular family prayer in your home, imagine the power you can have to bless your family if *you* organize it. Be a Nephi and take charge! Da-da-da-dat, da-dah! (That was the sound of a bugle playing *"Charge!"*)

GET IN THE HABIT

Evening prayers have never been a problem for me. I never forget. But there was a time, I'm embarrassed to admit, when I would forget, skip, or run out of time for my morning prayers. Finally I formed a habit. You need to find your own way, of course, but this is what I do. The instant I get up, I drop to my knees and pray. If I try to wait until I'm dressed, or showered, or something like that, I always seem to run out of time. So I say my prayers first thing.

That method works for me. You'll have to find one that works for you, but find one! You can't afford to miss that morning time with your Father in Heaven. Elder H. Burke Peterson shares with us how he formed a good habit:

> When I was a boy, I couldn't always remember to say my prayers at night. I wanted to, but sometimes I would forget because I'd be too sleepy. When I got older, I had a great idea.
>
> If I were you, I would go out in the field and find a

rock about the size of your fist. I'd wash it clean and put it under my pillow. Then, when I would get in bed at night and drop my head on my pillow—crack! I would remember to get out of bed and kneel down by it. I would then put the rock on the floor by my bed and go to sleep. Then, in the morning, I would jump out of bed, and as my foot would come down on the rock—"Ouch!" And I would remember to kneel down and say my morning prayers. Sometimes we need reminders to form good habits.[7]

Because of Bishop Peterson's talk, many young people throughout the Church have made "Prayer Rocks" to help them remember to pray. (Other ideas, like the ill-fated "Prayer Cactus," didn't catch on as well.)

SHOULD I ASK A BLESSING ON THE FOOD IN A RESTAURANT?

I love teenagers because they ask the most interesting questions! Do you bless the food when you're on a date? If you pray over your food in a public place, will it show your obedience to the principle of prayer, or might it just look like you are showing off? Elder Bruce R. McConkie wrote:

The practice of the Church in our day is to have family prayer twice daily, plus our daily personal prayers, plus a blessing on our food at mealtimes (except in those public or other circumstances where it would be ostentatious or inappropriate to do so), plus proper prayers in our meetings.[8]

There's a key. Be careful about praying in public if it feels inappropriate or ostentatious. Do you know what *ostentatious* means? Me neither. Just a second and I'll go look it up—ah ha, my dictionary says it means a "showy display." Yes, indeed. The "I'm-more-spiritual-than-you-are" display is not appropriate. So you'll just have to use your best judgment on this one. (My friend Brad Wilcox does what he calls the "Bayer Prayer." He bows his head and rubs his temples as if he has a headache that needs an aspirin, and offers a silent prayer on his food.)

THE BEST FOR LAST

As you know, the best place to learn about prayer—or any other subject, for that matter—is in the scriptures. So, to conclude this chapter, I'm going to include some classic scriptures about prayer. The Savior was an incredible teacher. He could teach great principles in just a few words. Listen to how beautifully Jesus taught the Nephites:

> And when thou prayest thou shalt not do as the hypocrites, for they love to pray, standing in the synagogues and in the corners of the streets, that they may be seen of men. Verily I say unto you, they have their reward.
>
> But thou, when thou prayest, enter into thy closet, and when thou hast shut thy door, pray to thy Father who is in secret; and thy Father, who seeth in secret, shall reward thee openly.
>
> But when ye pray, use not vain repetitions, as the heathen, for they think that they shall be heard for their much speaking.
>
> Be not ye therefore like unto them, for your Father knoweth what things ye have need of before ye ask him. (3 Nephi 13:5–8)

I have found that one of the best and fastest ways to get to know people is to ask them what their favorite scriptures are. These next verses are some of my very favorite. One of the first times I felt the Spirit, and *knew* I was feeling it, was when I was reading this passage of scripture. I was a sophomore in high school, and we were studying Church history and the Doctrine and Covenants in seminary. Just before bedtime one night, I was reading these verses in my Doctrine and Covenants:

> Pray always, and I will pour out my Spirit upon you, and great shall be your blessing—yea, even more than if you should obtain treasures of earth and corruptibleness to the extent thereof.
>
> Behold, canst thou read this without rejoicing and lifting up thy heart for gladness?
>
> Or canst thou run about longer as a blind guide?
>
> Or canst thou be humble and meek, and conduct thyself wisely before me? Yea, come unto me thy Savior. Amen. (D&C 19:38–41)

Did you catch that? You can become as rich as you want to in this world, but the Lord says will you have more joy if you will just "pray always." And can you read that without rejoicing? Wow. One of the weapons you'll need in your personal battles against Satan is prayer. Here's another great verse from the Doctrine and Covenants:

> Pray always, that you may come off conqueror; yea, that you may conquer Satan, and that you may escape the hands of the servants of Satan that do uphold his work. (D&C 10:5)

At the beginning of this chapter, we looked at James 1:5, the scripture that led Joseph Smith to pray. In James 1:6, it says: "But let him ask in faith, nothing wavering." We must learn to pray more earnestly, with more faith, with real intent, and with all of the energy and strength of our souls. Mormon taught, "Pray unto the Father with all the energy of heart" (Moroni 7:48).

Earlier, I joked about some of our half-hearted prayers—the "face-plant-in-the-mattress" thing. I'm embarrassed about those times when my prayers weren't with "real intent." Writing and researching for this chapter has helped me want to do better. I especially felt a new resolve to try harder when I read this beautiful counsel from Elder H. Burke Peterson:

As you feel the need to confide in the Lord or to improve the quality of your visits with him . . . may I suggest a process to follow: go where you can be alone, where you can think, where you can kneel, where you can speak out loud to him. The bedroom, the bathroom, or a closet will do. Now, picture him in your mind's eye. Think to whom you are speaking. Control your thoughts—don't let them wander. Address him as your Father and your friend. Now tell him things you really feel to tell him—not trite phrases that have little meaning, but have a sincere, heartfelt conversation with him. Confide in him. Ask him for forgiveness. Plead with him. Enjoy him. Thank him. Express your love to him. Then listen for his answers. Listening is an essential part of praying. Answers from the Lord come quietly, ever so quietly. In fact, few hear his answers audibly with their ears. We must be listening carefully or we will never recognize them. Most answers from the Lord are felt in our heart as a warm, comfortable expression, or they may come as thoughts to our mind. They come to those who are prepared and who are patient.[9]

I don't know if there is any way I can express how grateful I am that a fourteen-year-old boy offered a prayer in a sacred grove so many years ago. That prayer, and everything that has happened since, has changed my life. Because of that prayer, Samuel Alexander Pagan Kelsey and his wife, my fourth great-grandparents, crossed the plains and came to Utah. Because of that prayer, my father joined the Church when he was twenty-four years old. Because of that prayer, my brother David was given a powerful blessing with the priesthood of God before he underwent a kidney transplant.

Because of that prayer, I had the opportunity to serve a mission in the Philippines. Because of that prayer, I get to spend time with my favorite people in the world—wonderful teenagers like you. I am very, very grateful. Don't ever underestimate the power of prayer!

See you in Sixth Period!

EXTRA CREDIT

Prayer, various General Authorities (Salt Lake City: Deseret Book, 1977).

"Learning to Recognize Answers to Prayer," Richard G. Scott, *Ensign,* November 1989, pp. 30–32.

FIFTH PERIOD ENDNOTES

Division page quotation: Thomas S. Monson, *Ensign,* June 1986, p. 2.

1. Heber J. Grant, *Gospel Standards* (Salt Lake City: Improvement Era, 1942), p. 26.
2. H. Burke Peterson, *Ensign,* June 1981, p. 73; emphasis added.
3. Howard W. Hunter, *Ensign,* November 1977, p. 52.
4. *Words of Joseph Smith,* Andrew F. Ehat and Lyndon W. Cook, comp., eds. (Orem, Utah: Grandin Book Co., 1993), p. 15.
5. Ezra Taft Benson, *God, Family, Country* (Salt Lake City: Deseret Book, 1974), pp. 121–22.
6. Bruce R. McConkie, in *Prayer* (Salt Lake City: Deseret Book, 1977), p. 10.
7. H. Burke Peterson, *Ensign,* November 1981, p. 35.
8. Bruce R. McConkie, in *Prayer,* p. 12.
9. H. Burke Peterson, in *Prayer,* p. 108.

Geography 101
The Imagi-Nation

You see things and you say, "Why?" But I dream
things that never were, and I say, "Why not?"
—George Bernard Shaw

We're going on a trip! Yes, we're going to see another nation. It's not a European nation, or an African nation, but a nation more interesting and exciting than anything you've ever seen. Airfare is free, you never get jet lag, and you can be there in a second. In fact, you can leave whenever you want, on a moment's notice! You can go there when you're feeling bad, or when you're feeling glad. Where is this nation? It's in the "State of Mind" right there in your head. It's the *Imagi*-Nation.

The Imagi-Nation is your own private country. You own it! It's every bit as beautiful and exciting as you can—um—imagine. You've been there before, but you may have forgotten a few things.

Some people stop traveling to their Imagi-Nation as they get older. They say it's only for kids. They prefer a place they call "Reality." It's another nation in the State of Mind. Those who live there want everyone else to live there too. They say, "C'mon, get back to Reality."

Other people live in a place they call "The Past." You've probably heard someone say, "Hey, you're living in The Past!" Well, that's what they mean. It's the third nation in the State of Mind. Some people never seem to leave The Past. They don't try to go anywhere else, because they believe things will always be the way they've been in The Past. So they give up their passport, and never visit their Imagi-Nation. If you stay in The Past too long, you might get depressed. My advice is, don't live in The Past.

Where do most people live? I'm not sure. Probably in The Past with a daily commute to Reality. The most successful

119

and happy people in the world, however, young and old, spend a lot of time in their Imagi-Nation.

Imagi-Nation is divided into counties called "Dreams," cities called "Goals," and freeways called "Success." (Notice that "Success" is a freeway, not a city.) In Reality, freeways go from city to city, with a new city always ahead. In Imagi-Nation, Success means going from goal to goal, with a new goal always ahead! You can never see all of your Imagi-Nation, but boy-oh-boy, it's sure fun trying. No matter how far you travel, there's always more Imagi-Nation left!

There's something very special about your Imagi-Nation. You can bring things from there into Reality. In fact, almost everything you find in Reality came from Imagi-Nation. You can make the things you imagine become real; some people call this "making your dreams come true."

One day, a little boy was wandering around in his Imagi-Nation, and his teacher had to bring him back to Reality. It happened at the Jefferson School in Cedar Rapids in 1878. Miss Ida Palmer, the teacher, noticed a seven-year-old boy hunched over his desk fiddling with two pieces of wood. He was definitely somewhere in his Imagi-Nation. Miss Palmer asked him what he was doing. He answered "that he was assembling the parts of a flying machine, a larger version of which might enable him to fly with his brother." Miss Palmer knew the wonders of Imagi-Nation, so she didn't take the craft from the little boy, but she did tell him to come back to Reality. Later, Orville and his brother Wilbur visited Imagi-Nation again. And on December 17, 1903, the Wright Brothers flew a part of their Imagi-Nation into Reality.[1]

You too can make your dreams come true. If you can make it in your Imagi-Nation, you can make it in Reality. But, as with any trip, you have to do some planning. In Reality, you can go to a gas station and get a map to help you plan your journey, to make sure you don't miss the best stops along the way. There are plenty of gas stations in the

Imagi-Nation too, and they all have maps. Gas stations give us the fuel to travel, and maps tell us the best cities to visit. Gas stations are the Church, and maps are the gospel. The gospel map gives us a recommended tour, with stops along the way. You can visit any place you want in your Imagi-Nation, but the gospel map says, "Whatever you do, don't miss these cities!"

Some people travel without maps. They have no plans for their journey. It's unbelievable, but some people spend more time planning a picnic or a trip to the store than they do planning their whole lives! You, however, are different. You have a map with specific goals. And somewhere on your map there is a drawing of a compass that tells you where "north" is, that gives you direction. You see, some people live in their Imagi-Nation, but they go in the wrong direction. Big mistake.

What direction should we take when we enter our Imagi-Nation? I'll tell you: "Seek ye first the kingdom of God and his righteousness, and all these things shall be added unto you" (3 Nephi 13:33). That short scripture, which is also found in Matthew 6:33, is the greatest success formula there is. Seek the kingdom of God first. What good does it do to work hard and set and achieve goals if you're moving in the wrong direction? Set goals for graduating from seminary, for receiving your Young Women Recognition Award or Eagle Scout Badge. Then set goals for your mission, marriage in the temple, and education. When you move in the right direction, the Lord will help you achieve your goals. If you start now, by charting your course and living by a plan, you'll have a full and rich life with many exciting stops along the way!

In Reality, it's easy to tell when you've arrived at a new city. There's always a sign that says, "Welcome to _____." And in Imagi-Nation, it's easy to tell when you've reached a new goal. If you've set a goal to receive your Young Women

Recognition Award, or your Eagle Scout, there will come a time when you *know* you've achieved it. There are other kinds of goals that are harder to get a handle on. For example, what about the goal of being righteous? Can you suddenly check a box and say, "Okay, I'm righteous"? No. Why? Because righteousness is not that kind of goal. It's more like a way of life—a *direction,* or a mode of travel. You see, there are "do" goals, and there are "be" goals. Things that you *do,* you can check off when you're done. Things that you want to *be* are a little harder to measure, but they are still important.

Last semester, in *What I Wish I'd Known in High School: A Crash Course in Teenage Survival,* we talked mostly about "do" goals. This time we've been talking and will talk more about "be" goals, or direction goals. And that brings us to the next question:

ARE YOU EVERYTHING YOU WANT TO BE?

When I was only ten years old, I admired a sixth-grader in my elementary school very much. His name was Christian. He was always nice to everyone. He always seemed to be happy. He was outgoing, too. I'm not sure if I could have described why I admired him when I was ten, but now I know the right words. It's as simple as this: Christian was righteous. He was good. He glowed with the light of Christ. Can a twelve-year-old do that? You bet. Christian did. I wanted to be like that. I guess Christian was one of my first "role models."

Just before I entered seventh grade, my family moved to another part of town, but I never forgot about Christian. I still wanted to be like him. As the years went by, I remember writing down my feelings and goals from time to time, and when I did that I would think about Christian and other people I admired.

In junior high and high school, I found someone else to admire. He was outgoing and happy and good too, like

Christian. His name was Richard. Richard was popular—but unlike some of the others in the popular crowd, he was friendly with *all* the different social groups in the school, and everyone was friendly with him! Why? Because people of all kinds are drawn to goodness and righteousness. People are drawn to people who are happy. And nothing makes a person as happy as living the gospel can.

How about you? Is the person you *really* want to be hiding somewhere in your Imagi Nation? You can be that person in Reality if you really want to. People do it all the time. Let me tell you about Lynette from New Mexico. No, I have a better idea—I'll let *Lynette* tell you about Lynette! Let's read her letter together:

> As a freshman and sophomore I found myself in a clique which included myself and two other Mormon girls. Starting at a new school with new friends and a whole new life it seemed like the perfect answer, not to mention the fact that "cliques" give the feeling of stability and friendship from others in the group. Well, things seemed great at first, and high school couldn't be better until I learned more about the people in my clique and how others were looked down upon and pushed away by one of the girls in the group, which made the whole group look bad. Every day it would get worse and I would just stand there in silence, partly because I knew that it was "safe" in a clique and I didn't want to be an outcast. Things went on like this for the first two years of my high school life, and people at school were always nice to me when I was not with my friend who was always negative. Yet when I was around her I was looked at as a part of this group, and therefore I was also thought of as mean and negative.

Excuse me, but I need to interrupt and make a comment.

This is the point where Lynette started to ask, "Am I every-thing I want to be?" Okay, keep reading. *We now return you to your regularly scheduled letter:*

It wasn't until the summer before my junior year that I decided that the way things were going and the way people were being treated was not something I was willing to let keep happening. . . . I decided to break away and be my own person. Junior year began, and I slowly started to break away from the group, which was very difficult. But in the long run it was worth it. As I slowly broke away from the clique I decided that instead of joining a new one and having the same thing happen I would try some-thing else. From that day forward I promised myself and Heavenly Father that I would go to school every day and try my best to treat everyone (no matter who they are or what they look like) with the highest love and respect possible. Instead of joining a clique I would just be friends with everyone equally. I would go around to each individual clique and visit with people every day and talk to them and get to know them as my brothers and sisters and children of God.

I'm moving on to my senior year now, and my life couldn't be better. This past year has been filled with trials and struggles, yet with the wonderful friend-ships that I have built with people—being able to see them for who and what they are—those trials have been so much easier to handle and conquer. Life just seems to take on a new meaning.

I must admit that it wasn't easy to break away from security and comfort, even for an outgoing person (which is how I consider myself). Not having a best friend in the world can be hard at times, when you need a shoulder to cry on. But in the end I can guar-antee you that when you are nice and a friend to

> everyone, as opposed to just those in your little
> clique, life will be so much better and can bring you
> so much more joy than you'll ever know. There are
> so many wonderful people out there who are just
> waiting for a friend.

Isn't that great? Lynette took a hard look at herself, and at her life, and asked, "Am I everything I want to be?" And the answer was "no." So she changed. She put The Past behind her, she saw what she wanted in her Imagi-Nation, and she brought it into Reality.

Well, are *you* everything *you* want to be? How would you like to be different? If you can see it in your Imagi-Nation, you can make it in Reality. One of the cop-outs we hear all the time is: "That's just the way I am." If you're like me, whenever you hear someone say that, you want to respond, "No, you're just the way you've *chosen* to be." I know people who seem to be happy all the time, and yet they have major trials and difficulties in their lives. How do they do that? Well, at some point, those people made a conscious decision to be happy no matter what. They no longer say things like "He makes me so mad" or "This weather depresses me." They have taken control of their feelings.

On top of your TV or VCR, there's probably a remote control. With a remote control, you can "control" your TV from a "remote" location. If the TV is too loud, you can turn the volume down or even push the "mute" button. (I've tried pointing the remote at people in my apartment and pushing the "mute" button when they get too loud, but it doesn't work.)

When you let others control how you feel, it is as if you have given out a remote control that has a button on it for each of your moods. If you walk past someone in the hall, and they don't say "hi," do you let that affect your mood? If so, you have given away your remote control—and as long as you let others keep it, they will keep affecting your moods. Does that make sense?

Some people give their remote controls to the dumbest things. For example, would you give a personal remote control to the Big Dipper? Some people have. It's called astrology. "Gee, I'd better check my horoscope to see what's going to happen to me today, so I'll know what kind of a mood to be in." Yup, they have given a remote control to big balls of burning gas billions of miles away. Brilliant move. These people are not living in Reality or the Imagi-Nation. It's more like the "Halluci-Nation."

Anyway, here's the point: You need self-control, not remote control. *Take back the remote!* If you want to make a major stride forward as a teenager, decide now that you will be the kind of person you want to be, and that you will stop blaming everyone and everything outside of you for your moods and circumstances. Of course there are trials in life, but there are a million examples of people who have succeeded in spite of their trials. You can too! Or you can (as many people do) blame the government, high taxes, bad weather, your family, your genes, your teacher, your luck, your birth order, or the Big Dipper for your problems.

I have a friend named Greg. I heard him teach a class once in which he shared his amazing personal story of "taking back the remote." I should start by saying that Greg looks like one of those guys on the cover of a J. Crew catalog. No exaggeration. I wouldn't know, but the girls all say he's "gorgeous." Now you'll understand why this story was so amazing to me.

Greg told of a time back in his early high school years when he had no friends and was very overweight. He didn't feel all that good about himself, and he just kind of moved along through life like everyone else. One day something interesting happened. There was a popular girl at his school who walked up to Greg and simply said, "Greg, are you everything you want to be?" (That's where I got the idea for this part of the book!) Deep inside, Greg answered to himself, "no." He knew he could be better. This simple question from a wise young woman served as a wake-up call for Greg. He knew he was more than he was demonstrating. Greg took back the remote. All that summer, he worked. He exercised like crazy and lost a lot of weight. He changed his diet and built up some muscle by working out. When Greg went back to school in the fall, he looked totally different. Nobody recognized him! They thought he was a new kid who had just moved in. He made a lot of friends, and soon became one of the most popular boys at the school.

Greg explained humbly that he kind of got caught up in his newfound popularity. After a while, unfortunately, he wasn't treating people as well as he should have. Once again, this amazing young woman came to Greg and asked him the same question: "Greg, are you everything you want to be?" And once again, Greg answered "no." He looked deep inside. He had already changed his appearance, but perhaps there was more remodeling to be done. Now he had to work on his heart. He decided he would talk to everyone, not just those in the popular group, and he would start treating everyone with kindness and respect. And he did!

I really love this story. It happened because a young woman consistently asked that wonderful question: "Are you everything you want to be?" and because an honest young man was willing to answer the question, then take charge and change what needed to be changed.

DAILY REMINDERS

How do we make sure we're going in the right direction as we travel through the Imagi-Nation? Well, asking ourselves certain questions every day, like the one Greg's friend asked, can really help. In my own life, I try to remind myself *every day* of certain things. On my bathroom mirror, I have a picture of the *Christus,* the beautiful statue of the Savior in the Temple Square visitors' center. Underneath it are printed the words, "He is so powerful." This is a daily reminder to me to have faith in Jesus Christ. I love him, and I know that he has the power and the will to order all things for my good as fast as I am able to receive them. (See D&C 111:11.)

Daily reminders help keep us moving in the right direction. One of the reasons we're told to read the scriptures *every day* is because doing so will allow the Spirit of the Lord to be with us *every day*. The same applies to daily prayers.

May I suggest a daily reminder that you might like to use? I was once watching a television show about the Notre Dame football team. When the team leaves the locker room to go out onto the playing field, they go down a long staircase. Above the stairs is a sign that reads, "Play like a champion today." Each player, as he goes down the stairs, reaches up and touches the sign. Why? you ask. Because just *looking* at the sign might not have the same impact as touching it. Touching the sign forces them to concentrate and internalize the message, *"Play like a champion today!"*

I love this idea, and I've thought about it a lot. I thought about how I might make a similar sign, and I remembered a classic talk given by Presiding Bishop Robert D. Hales. He said:

> As a young man, I had an opportunity to serve in the U.S. Air Force as a jet-fighter pilot. Each unit in our squadron had a motto that would inspire its efforts. Our unit motto—displayed on the side of our aircraft—was "Return with Honor." This motto was a constant reminder to us of our determination to return to our home base with honor only after having expended all of our efforts to successfully complete every aspect of our mission.

This same motto, "Return with Honor," can be applied to each of us in our eternal plan of progression. Having lived with our Heavenly Father and having come to earth life, we must have determination to return with honor to our heavenly home.[1]

I think it would be a wonderful idea if each of us displayed a "Return with Honor" sign in our room, right next to the light switch so we would see it every day when we left. We could even touch the sign when we leave, and have the conviction to return not only to heaven, but to our bedroom each night as clean as we were when we left in the morning. Actually, if you were here with me right now, you would see two signs on my wall: "PLAY LIKE A CHAMPION TODAY" and "RETURN WITH HONOR." These daily reminders inspire me and help me to stay on course and heading in the right direction.

The nice people at Deseret Book went to work and inserted a "Return with Honor" sign at the end of this chapter that you can use in your room. Just cut along the dotted line and hang it right up there. And you can add your own daily reminders if you want!

SUMMARY

I've told you about some of the people I admire—people like Christian, Richard, Lynette, and Greg. I'm sure you have a list of your own. And who knows—I'll bet there's someone out there watching and admiring and learning from you! So do your best and don't let them down.

If you're living in The Past, now is the time to stop! The wonderful message of the gospel is that you can change, and repent, and be better every day. We all have to come back to Reality from time to time, but make sure you spend a lot of time in your Imagi-Nation. Are you everything you want to be? Not yet? That's okay; most people aren't. But you can get to work on it.

You know better than anyone else in the world what your weaknesses are. You also know better than anyone else in the world how much better you could be if you really tried. I know you've had moments when you've thought about trying to be better. You know that, don't you. Will this be the day that you decide to be better than you've ever been before? Will this be the day that you actually believe what prophets have said about you and your generation? Will this be the day that you begin to be the way you've always known you can be? As Robert Louis Stevenson said, "You cannot run away from weakness. You must sometime fight it out or perish, and if that be so, why not now, and where you stand?" What a penetrating question: *"Why not now?"* Why not, when you're finished reading this chapter, get out a paper and pencil and write down all the things you want to become! Why not now? Design the kind of life you want, visualize the kind of person you want to be in your Imagi-Nation, and you can make it happen in Reality!

EXTRA CREDIT

As a Man Thinketh, James Allen (New York: Barnes & Noble Inc., 1992).

SIXTH PERIOD ENDNOTES

1. Tom D. Crouch, *The Bishop's Boys: A Life of Wilbur and Orville Wright* (New York: W. W. Norton & Co., 1989), p. 57.

2. Robert D. Hales, *Ensign,* May 1990, p. 39.

RETURN WITH HONOR

College Prep 101

Preparing for the Temple:
The University of the Lord

It is the deepest desire of my heart to have every member of the Church worthy to enter the temple.
—Howard W. Hunter

Seventh Period

If someone were to ask you, "Where is your very favorite place in the whole world?" how would you answer? When I was younger, I might have answered, "Disneyland" or "camping in the mountains" or maybe "an air show" (I love airplanes).

But now I know a better place. There is no place like it. It is "out of this world." It's the closest thing to being in the celestial kingdom that we have. In fact, a certain room within it actually represents the celestial kingdom. Telestial things are missing from this building. You could search the whole structure and not find a television, a radio, or a Nintendo. The worldly noise disappears as you enter. The sounds of the city, the traffic, and the hustle and bustle are left behind.

The moment you walk through the front doors, you are engulfed in a feeling of peace and quiet. Suddenly, the world is gone. Friendly, smiling faces greet you around every corner. People speak in whispers. The surroundings are bright and light and spotless. You exchange your worldly costume for white clothes, and you sit in a small chapel for a while as an organist softly plays a few hymns.

Whenever I go to the temple, I hear myself say, "I *love* this place." And I really do. It is heaven on earth—the closest thing to heaven we have. Sitting there in my white clothes, feeling clean inside and out, *is* heaven. And it feels like being home with God. It is his holy place, his holy house. Elder Bruce R. McConkie taught:

> When the Lord comes from heaven to the earth, as
> he does more frequently than is supposed, where

135

does he make his visitations? Those whom he visits know the answer; he comes to one of his houses. Whenever the Great Jehovah visits his people, he comes, suddenly as it were, to his temple.[1]

The temple is holy because it is literally the House of the Lord. It is also holy because of what we do there. We seal families together. Our hearts are turned to our fathers and mothers, and their hearts are turned to us. It is holy because we perform ordinances there for those who have died. Many, many people have lived and died on this earth without having received baptism. Many have married and raised children but were not sealed to them. We who are living can do this work for them in the temple. The work is very important to those who have died, and we serve them by doing it for them. One day, we will greet those people, and the reunion will be wonderful.

Horace Cummings recorded: "Concerning the work for the dead, [Joseph] said that in the resurrection those who had been worked for would fall at the feet of those who had done their work, kiss their feet, embrace their knees and manifest the most exquisite gratitude."[2]

WHAT DOES "ENDOWMENT" MEAN?

In addition to performing baptisms for the dead and other proxy ordinances, in the temple we receive our "endowment." An *endowment* is a gift, and the temple endowment is a gift from heaven. We never talk about the specifics of the endowment, because it is sacred. Many misunderstand this concept and think it is "secret." Let me see if I can explain. Have you ever had someone make fun of something that was really important to you? I think we've all had that experience, and it can hurt very much. I can't think of anything that I consider more sacred than my understanding and feelings about the temple. It is simply not right to talk about the specifics of the temple anywhere but within its walls.

Wouldn't it feel strange if you attended a stake conference, and after singing a hymn and opening with prayer, the speakers discussed the National Football League or R.V. maintenance? It just doesn't fit! We don't talk about the endowment outside of the temple because it's simply too sacred for common conversation. It doesn't feel right to talk about it just anywhere. It doesn't fit.

There are some general things we can appropriately discuss, though. President Howard W. Hunter taught, "Let us share with our children the spiritual feelings we have in the temple. And let us teach them more earnestly and more comfortably the things we can appropriately say about the purposes of the house of the Lord."[3] I'd like to try to do that.

One of the basic things to understand about the temple is that it is a place of instruction. In fact, the temple has sometimes been called "The University of the Lord." Elder James E. Talmage wrote:

> This course of instruction includes a recital of the most prominent events of the creative period, the condition of our first parents in the Garden of Eden, their disobedience and consequent expulsion from that blissful abode, their condition in the lone and dreary world when doomed to live by labor and sweat, the plan of redemption by which the great transgression may be atoned, the period of the great apostasy, the restoration of the Gospel with all its ancient powers and privileges, the absolute and indispensable condition of personal purity and devotion to the right in present life, and a strict compliance with Gospel requirements.[4]

As you can see, there's a lot to learn! President Howard W. Hunter taught, "As we attend the temple, we learn more richly and more deeply the purpose of life and the atoning sacrifice of the Lord Jesus Christ."[5] It's true. As a nineteen-year-old preparing for a mission, I remember some of my first impressions after I received my endowment. One of them was, "Wow. The plan of salvation is a lot more organized than I thought." And it is.

In the temple, along with the instruction, we are also given what President Joseph Fielding Smith called "keys":

> Sons and daughters have access to the home where [Father in Heaven] dwells, and you cannot receive that access until you go to the temple. Why? Because you must receive certain key words as well as make covenants by which you are able to enter. If you try to get into the house, and the door is locked, how are you going to enter, if you haven't your key? You get your key in the temple, which will admit you.[6]

In probably the most specific and most often quoted statement about the endowment ever given, President Brigham Young said:

> Your endowment is, to receive all those ordinances in the house of the Lord, which are necessary for you, after you have departed this life, to enable you to walk back to the presence of the Father, passing the angels who stand as sentinels, being enabled to give them the key words, the signs and tokens, pertaining to the holy Priesthood, and gain your eternal exaltation in spite of earth and hell.[7]

As President Joseph Fielding Smith mentioned, we make covenants with the Lord in the temple. A covenant is a two-way agreement. You are already familiar with the covenant of the sacrament. We covenant to always remember him and to keep his commandments, and in return, the Lord promises that the saints will have his spirit to be with them. What covenants do we make in the temple? Good question. I'll let President Ezra Taft Benson answer that one:

> In the course of our visits to the temple, we are given insights into the meaning of the eternal journey of man. We see beautiful and impressive symbolisms of the most important events—past, present, and future—symbolizing man's mission in relationship to God. We are reminded of our obligations as we make solemn covenants pertaining to obedience, consecration, sacrifice, and dedicated service to our Heavenly Father.[8]

HOW DO I PREPARE?

I think I've said as much as I can about what we learn and do within the temple. The more important question for us now is, "How do I prepare?" At the beginning of this chapter, you read the words of President Howard W. Hunter. Let's read more of what he said:

> It would be the deepest desire of my heart to have every member of the Church be temple worthy. I would hope that every adult member would be worthy of—and carry—a current temple recommend, even if proximity to a temple does not allow immediate or frequent use of it.[9]

We often use the word *someday* when we refer to the temple: "Someday I will go to the temple," or "Someday I'll be married in the house of the Lord." And that's okay. But President Hunter seems to be saying, "Yes, someday you will. But be *worthy* to enter the temple *right now*." We should strive to live our lives so that we would *always* be worthy to enter the temple, instead of just becoming worthy "someday." That was President Hunter's challenge—for every member of the Church to be temple worthy, whether they're at the temple or not.

Being worthy "right now" is one of the main things we've talked about in this book. We're not interested in the "pre-planned sin and repentance" idea, or the "I'll do what I want now and prepare for the temple and a mission later" idea. We want to be valiant *right now*. And we want to continue being valiant all our lives, so that, if we are called to go home sooner than expected, we can "look up" when we're brought to stand before God. (See Alma 5:19.)

One way you can try to be worthy of the temple right now is to try to make your home like the temple. Does that sound like a strange idea? Grab your scriptures, and let's look up "Temple" in the Bible Dictionary (it comes right after the Topical Guide in the LDS edition of the Bible). Here's what it says:

> A temple is literally a house of the Lord, a holy sanctuary in which sacred ceremonies and ordinances of the gospel are performed by and for the living and also in behalf of the dead. A place where the Lord may come, it is the most holy of any place of worship on the earth. Only the home can compare with the temple in sacredness.

Whoa—did you hear that? *Only the home can compare with the temple in sacredness.* The implications of that are staggering. For example, do you watch TV shows at home that you wouldn't dare show in the chapel or at the stake center? Well, according to our Bible Dictionary, the home is *more* sacred than the chapel or stake center. I think many of us (myself included) have watched things at home that we wouldn't feel comfortable showing at church. Oops.

If you read my last book, you know that I've become an anti-television kind of guy. But I'm not alone. President Gordon B. Hinckley counseled: "I am suggesting that we spend a little less time in idleness, in the fruitless pursuit of watching some inane and empty television programs. Time so utilized can be put to better advantage, and the consequences will be wonderful. Of that I do not hesitate to assure you."[10] If you would not allow "empty and inane" television programs into the temple, then the home is too sacred a place for them too. You see, when you walk into the temple, your brain walks in with you. All of your memories, everything you've seen on TV, including the things you wish you hadn't seen, go with you. You don't want those memories walking onto the stage of your mind when you're in the temple. If we have the goal of being prepared for the temple on our minds every day, it will help us choose what we should watch and what we shouldn't. And, of course, if that's true of television, it must be true of the music we listen to as well. Those tunes and lyrics walk into the temple with us too.

How else can we make our home more like the temple? Well, would you shout and quarrel with your brothers and sisters in the chapel? No way. You would be a little quieter, a little more patient, and a little more forgiving. Therefore, to prepare for the temple *right now*, we could be a little quieter, a little more patient, and a little more forgiving *right now*.

In short, the way to prepare for the temple is to live the gospel. Make your home as peaceful as the celestial room at the temple—a place where everyone is comfortable, where no one is threatened by the criticism or harsh words of other family members, where there is peace and happiness and prayer. Can you do this all by yourself? Of course not. But what you can do will affect every other member of your family. You can always have the temple in the back of your mind as a model for what you want your home to be.

Earlier in this book we talked about "daily reminders."

President Spencer W. Kimball gave us advice on a daily reminder for the temple:

> It seems to me it would be a fine thing if every set of parents would have in every bedroom in their house a picture of the temple so the boy or girl from the time he is an infant could look at the picture every day and it becomes a part of his life. When he reaches the age that he needs to make this very important decision, it will have already been made.[11]

Maybe we could put our "Return with Honor" sign next to a picture of the temple. Of all the goals you set in life, one of the most important is that you marry in the temple. President Howard W. Hunter taught, "Let us make the temple, with temple worship and temple covenants and temple marriage, our ultimate earthly goal and the supreme mortal experience."[12]

Somewhere out there is your future husband or wife. What do you suppose they are up to these days? Hopefully, they have a picture of the temple on their wall, and they're anticipating being in the temple on their wedding day. Hopefully, they have as their "ultimate earthly goal" being in the temple with you. And hopefully, they're concentrating on being worthy right now, not just "someday."

As you may have already figured out, I'm single. I've been to the temple many times, but one day, I'll be taking my fiancée with me. I don't know who she is yet. I wonder where she is, and what she's doing! Maybe she had a date last night. Did she return home with honor? Is she dating young men who respect her standards, who honor their priesthood? Does she love the Young Women's Values? I think she does.

I can't wait to meet her. I want to be the best I can for her. I can't wait to take her to the temple. I have something I want to say to her that I have been planning for years. I'm sorry to get so personal, but I can't think of any other way to let you know how I feel about the temple. A temple marriage has always been my goal. I have never even considered getting married anywhere else.

What am I going to say? Well, I'll tell you part of it. I want to look across the altar and say, "I loved you before I even met you." What do I mean by that? Well, the best way I can show my love for my future wife is to keep myself clean right now. Every time I honor the law of chastity, in words or thoughts or actions, I'm saying, "I love you." Every time I refuse to watch an immoral TV show or movie, every time I'm on a date and I am careful in my thoughts and expressions of affection, I'm saying, "I love you." I'm saying it to the Lord, who has asked me to keep it, and I'm also saying it to my future wife.

When you're married, you're supposed to say "I love you" every day. Well, I've been saying "I love you" to my wife for many years, although she hasn't been there to hear it. One day I'll find her, and we'll walk into a sealing room in the house of the Lord. Then we'll kneel across a holy altar, and I'll hold her hand, and tell her face to face. It will be a wonderful day.

Hang on a second while I dry my eyes. (Sniff, sniff.) Okay. So, how do you prepare for the temple? Well, whether you like it or not, you *are* preparing for the temple. Preparing for the temple isn't something you do "someday," it's something you're doing right now! And your future spouse is preparing too. You can prepare well, or you can prepare poorly. Everything you are doing now, you will take with you to your first temple recommend interview. So I challenge you to keep out of your house anything that you wouldn't want in the house of the Lord, because whatever you allow into your home will be carried into the temple by your memory. Make the temple your "ultimate earthly goal," and love your future spouse by keeping the commandments.

As I'm sitting here writing this, I have a current temple recommend in my back pocket. I hope I will always have a temple recommend in my back pocket. Whatever other worldly things I keep in there, along with all the plastic and identification, I always want to have this celestial "activity card" for the University of the Lord. One day you will go to the temple too. I don't know if I'll ever meet you in the celestial room, but let's do all we can to meet one day in the place that room represents: the celestial kingdom.

I hope you can see that everything we've discussed in this book has led us up to this chapter on the temple. How can we be temple worthy right now? Well, let's adopt the "I-want-to-be-valiant" attitude. Let's keep our hands clean and our hearts pure. Let's repent of our sins. Let's you and I strive to recognize and keep the Spirit as we pray with more faith. Let us imagine the kind of person we can be and bring it into reality. Let us go to the temple with honor, and return with honor to our Father in heaven.

Our second semester is ending, and I have to tell you, this has really been fun. It sounds a little corny, but I'll miss talking to you! I imagine wonderful teenagers like you in my mind as I write, and I'll miss you! I hope as soon as you put this book down, you'll go out and pick up another one. I know you're already reading your scriptures daily, so I mean another book. A television substitute. A book that will uplift you and inspire you and teach you something. You are wonderful, my friend! Thanks for attending the second semester—I hope you got answers to some of your "deep-down" questions. Hang in there, keep the faith, and I'll talk to you again soon! 'Bye!

EXTRA CREDIT

Why Say No When the World Says Yes?, Randal A. Wright, comp. (Salt Lake City: Deseret Book, 1993).

The Mountain of the Lord, videocassette (Salt Lake City: The Church of Jesus Christ of Latter-day Saints, 1993.

SEVENTH PERIOD ENDNOTES

Division page quotation: Howard W. Hunter, *Ensign,* November 1994, p. 8.

1. Bruce R. McConkie, *The Mortal Messiah,* 4 vols. (Salt Lake City: Deseret Book, 1979–81), 1:98–99.
2. Truman G. Madsen, *Joseph Smith the Prophet* (Salt Lake City: Bookcraft, 1989), p. 99.
3. Howard W. Hunter, *Ensign,* November 1994, p. 88.
4. James E. Talmage, *The House of the Lord* (Salt Lake City: Deseret Book, 1968), pp. 83–84.
5. Howard W. Hunter, *Ensign,* November 1994, p. 88.
6. Joseph Fielding Smith Jr., *Doctrines of Salvation,* 3 vols. (Salt Lake City: Bookcraft, 1955), 2:40.
7. *Discourses of Brigham Young,* sel. John A. Widtsoe (Salt Lake City: Deseret Book, 1954), p. 416.
8. *The Teachings of Ezra Taft Benson* (Salt Lake City: Bookcraft, 1988), p. 251.
9. Howard W. Hunter, *Ensign,* July 1994, p. 5.
10. Gordon B. Hinckley, *Ensign,* May 1995, p. 88.
11. *The Teachings of Spencer W. Kimball,* Edward L. Kimball, ed. (Salt Lake City: Bookcraft, 1982), p. 301.
12. Howard W. Hunter, *Ensign,* November 1994, p. 88.